Classic

AYR UNITED

FOOTBALL CLUB

Classics

AYR UNITED

FOOTBALL CLUB

DUNCAN CARMICHAEL

TEMPUS

Acknowledgements

In compiling this book, particular help was needed in the matter of tracking down many of the illustrations which have been used. For providing that material, and granting permission for its use, I am most grateful to the following people and organisations: Brian Caldwell, John Dalton, Kenneth Ferguson Photography, Les Flannigan, Craig Halkett of the *Daily Record*, Alan Hammond, Tim Harrison, Stewart McConnell, Kenny Ramsay of *The Sun*, Mike Wilson of *The Ayr Advertiser*, *The Ayrshire Post* and the SNS Group.

I am further grateful to the directors of Ayr United Football Club for giving an official endorsement to this publication and for allowing the club badge to be reproduced. I am even more grateful to succeeding generations of Ayr United teams for producing so many great memories.

The support of my family was never going to be in question and I thank my wife, Carol, daughter, Jill, and son, David, for that. Yet their support for this project was insignificant in comparison to their support for the club. We had a summer holiday in Whitley Bay because Ayr United were playing in a nearby tournament at Blyth Spartans! The Carmichael family did not even remotely consider an alternative holiday in a sun-spot. It has to be acknowledged, too, that there are others who can match, and even exceed, such an example of dedication to the club. This depth of feeling compounds the need to record the history.

Frontispiece: The club nickname 'The Honest Men' derives from Burns. Rabbie would have approved of the neckwear! *Kenneth Ferguson Photography*

First published 2002

Tempus Publishing Limited
The Mill, Brimscombe Port,
Stroud, Gloucestershire, GL5 2QG

Copyright © Duncan Carmichael, 2002

British Library Cataloguing in Publication Data.
A catalogue record for this book is available from the British Library.

ISBN 0 7524 2439 4

Typesetting and origination by Tempus Publishing Limited
Printed in Great Britain by Midway Colour Print, Wiltshire

Gordon Dalziel, the club's second longest serving manager of all time.

Introduction

It may well seem that a book on *Ayr United Classic Matches* has been written in response to the bold cup deeds of the year 2002. Alas, no. The timing of this book is coincidental. Yet it is a happy coincidence. There really could not have been a better time to record details of the finest matches. In retrospect, perhaps the expression 'classic matches' should be qualified to read 'classic matches or occasions'. There are last-day relegation escapes contained herein. Yes, they were great occasions; but they were also occasions when desperation was a far more important priority than flowing football.

In the matter of selecting matches for inclusion, the only problem that arose was being spoiled for choice. In cup competitions, it is traditionally defined as a shock when a club eliminates a club from a higher League. However, in Ayr United's case, it is not even a mild surprise when this happens. To suggest this is not tantamount to arrogance. It can be substantiated in fact. The sheer number of 'supposed' shocks that have occurred in Ayr's history meant that a certain amount of difficulty was experienced in choosing what to include.

It was a curious coincidence that some of the most worthy matches were taking place while this book was being prepared. Ayr United supporters will now be highly familiar with the road to Hampden. These great occasions are well worth recording for posterity and so too are the older matches, some of which are outwith living memory.

Of course, great matches produce equally great heroes, such as Andy Walker, who gently chipped the ball into the Kilmarnock net from the penalty spot; Gerry Phillips, for his saving goal in a last-game relegation escape; John Gallacher, for his famous Christmas Eve penalty save against Rangers; Peter Price, whose goalscoring statistics resemble fiction; and Willie Japp, who scored the most famous miskicked goal in the history of the club. The stories of these, and so many more, heroes are recounted in the pages ahead.

In the interests of accuracy, details have been authenticated, where possible, by reference to several reports. The author has also attended a large proportion of the matches covered, so it has been possible to write from the first-hand perspective of a fan. This fan bias has ensured that defeats are few in the pages ahead. However, it was necessary to cover some on the premise that the occasion was too big to be excluded.

An unreserved apology is hereby extended to any supporter whose favourite Ayr United memory is not contained within these pages. It is confidently aniticipated that few, if any, will require that apology.

FALKIRK v. AYR UNITED

8 September 1913
Brockville Park

·Scottish League First Division

When Ayr FC amalgamated with Parkhouse in 1910, there was no discernible opposition despite the fact that the town's two Second Division clubs had been experiencing a co-existence in which the rivalry was bitter to the point of blind hatred. Hindsight is always 100 per cent accurate and, on that basis, it can be stated that the amalgamation process was agreed with both clubs labouring under the misapprehension that a newly-formed Ayr United FC would immediately be voted into the First Division. This optimism proved to be a hoax, although the new club did succeed in finishing second in the Second Division table of 1910/11. In 1911/12, the championship was won, yet still the club failed in a bid for election to the top sphere. After retaining the Second Division title in 1912/13, the club at last succeeded in being voted into the First Division.

The transition was traumatic as the first four League fixtures were all lost. Further ignominy was then experienced with a 1-0 defeat away to Stevenston United in the first round of the Scottish Qualifying Cup. At this time, Stevenston United played in the same League as Ayr United Reserves. Two days after what remains one of the most shameful results in the club's history, it was then necessary to play at Falkirk in the League. At this time, Falkirk were the Scottish Cup holders. The prospect was daunting.

This match was played on a Monday, the occasion of a local Falkirk holiday, with a kick-off time of 3.30 p.m. A contingent of Ayr United supporters left Ayr on the 12.25 p.m. train and it arrived at Glasgow St Enoch at 2.10 p.m. rather than the scheduled arrival time of 1.55 p.m. This meant that the 2.10 p.m. train from Glasgow Queen Street to Falkirk was missed. On their eventual arrival at the Falkirk ground, the latecomers were given scarcely believ-able news by the visiting supporters. 'Yin-nane for United' was the gist of it.

The information was accurate, McGowan having scored in the eighth minute with a shot that entered the Falkirk net via an upright. Immediately, the home side set about the task of making Ayr United pay for such an impertinence. Their opportunity came when Willie McStay brought down Croall at the cost of a penalty kick. Croall, formerly of the aforemen-tioned Parkhouse, took the kick himself, only to be denied by a save from Sam Herbertson. An eyewitness account related that this was 'to the great delight of the small Ayr coterie'. In football parlance, it remains common to describe a goalkeeper as a hero after a penalty save but, within two years of this match, Herbertson was a hero in the true sense. At the age of twenty-six, he was killed in action whilst fighting at Gallipoli as a Royal Scots Fusilier.

The Ayr cause became heavily handicapped when Billy Middleton fell heavily to the ground while vying for possession. He took no further part in the match, so Ayr United were numerically disadvantaged with an hour of playing time left. Sensing blood, Falkirk laid siege to the Ayr goal, only to become frustrated by a disallowed effort and the continued reflexes of Herbertson.

In the second half, the Brockville Park incline favoured the 'Falkirk Bairns'. Immediately, the balance of play also favoured the eager home players. Typifying the onslaught on Herbertson was a save in which he ended up with Croall and Terris on top of him. Then, in a breakaway, McGowan beat home full-back Morrison before putting Ayr United's ten men 2-0 ahead with an oblique drive. The goal was scored on fifty-two minutes and it is on record that: 'The few Ayr supporters again gave a demonstration of their phenomenally strong vocal powers'.

Falkirk 1
McCulloch

Ayr United 3
McGowan (2), Goodwin

Hilly Goodwin.

Billy Middleton.

Almost predictably, the attacking efforts of Falkirk became increasingly desperate, although, in another breakaway, Hilly Goodwin was downed in the penalty area when clear through on the home goal. A penalty kick was claimed but denied. Perhaps in frustration, full-back Morrison showed his forwards how to attack. In a dribbling move, he could not be stopped and eventually passed to McCulloch, who lashed the ball past Herbertson. The goal time was sixty-nine minutes and the loss of this goal was a matter of great concern. This concern was compounded when Falkirk continued to attack in pursuit of an equaliser. Strenuous efforts were to no avail and what happened next was in keeping with the general trend of the game. In another breakaway, Hilly Goodwin drew the goalkeeper before firing the ball into the net. Or, to put it into 1913 terminology, he drew the goalkeeper before propelling the spheroid into the rigging. Yet it was 3-1 to Ayr United however you looked at it, and it was reported that: 'The Ayr people made a great demonstration of this third success'. Fourteen minutes remained, and the Ayr team even made so bold as to gain the ascendancy.

It was correctly pointed out that: 'The victory provided one of the biggest surprises ever sprung upon the football public, and inside three days the Ayr United team have supplied two sensational results. Half an hour of Monday's form would have accounted for Stevenston United'. When the result was wired to Ayr, many supporters had difficulty in believing it. One of them even telephoned a source in Glasgow for verification. Goalkeeper Sam Herbertson played a key role, most notably with his penalty save. In view of his looming demise in the First World War, it seems fitting to dedicate this account to his memory.

Falkirk: Stewart, Morrison, Sharp, Gibbons, Henderson, Reilly, McNaught, McCulloch, Robertson, Croall and Terris.

Ayr United: Herbertson, 'Campbell', McStay, McDougall, Quinn, Baxter, McKinnell, Robertson, A.H. Goodwin, McGowan and Middleton.

Rangers v. Ayr United

13 February 1915   Scottish League First Division
Ibrox Park

This was the first instance of two brothers playing in the same Ayr United team. Inside forward Jacky Goodwin had played for the club in the early part of the inaugural season, prior to a transfer to Rangers in November 1910. He returned in April 1914, by which time his brother, Hilly Goodwin, (actual name Alex Hill Goodwin) had lost his first-team place and was consigned to playing for the reserves. For the trip to Ibrox in February 1915, wing-half Jack Nevin was unavailable for selection and, therefore, Hilly was drafted in. The captain of Ayr United at this time was Willie McStay, although he was still at the tender age of twenty. He was in the midst of a long-term loan stay from Celtic, yet he did not come in for any 'special' treatment from the home support. Two years later, almost to the day, an Ayr United game at Ibrox was the occasion of Jimmy Hay, by then the Ayr captain, becoming heavily barracked for being a former Celtic player. Both players had illustrious Celtic careers, but the crucial difference was that Willie McStay was still on the threshold of stardom.

As the war progressed, travelling restrictions became more acute, but the Ayr United supporters heading for Glasgow experienced no difficulties in travelling by rail. It was generally estimated that they numbered several hundred and, though this did not constitute an especially large support, it was reported that: 'When the teams took the field, the volume of sound that greeted the visitors was highly gratifying.'

Willie McStay won the toss and elected to play with the wind. The advantage of this quickly proved to be considerable with the Rangers defence being well tested. Then came a threat to that attacking momentum when Joe Cassidy injured himself while putting in a tackle. Play stopped for a full minute to allow him to be assisted off and the next major development came when the Ayr team was still a man short. That was after twenty-six minutes, when Billy Middleton got the ball near the touchline and sent in a low cross which was dummied by Jacky Goodwin to allow Jimmy Richardson the opportunity to calmly go around goalkeeper Kelso and deposit the ball in the corner of the Rangers net. Just after this, Joe Cassidy reappeared and almost immediately sent a scorching drive over the crossbar.

At the approach of half-time, clever play developed on the Ayr right but the move threatened to be broken up when home full-back Craig attempted a clearance. Luckily it was a hashed attempt, which allowed Jacky Goodwin to get possession. He evaded a tackle and then parted with the ball, only to have it returned from Billy Middleton. Jacky Goodwin parted with the ball again – right into the back of Herbert Lock's net! With forty-two minutes on the clock, it was Rangers 0 Ayr United 2. The beaten Rangers goalkeeper would find himself being loaned out to Ayr United at a later stage of the war (September 1917 until February 1918). This player had entrepreneurial skills as well as goalkeeping skills. In August 1919, he opened a fish and chip shop in Copland Road, right next to Ibrox Park.

A threat to Ayr United's two-goal cushion was the wind that had to be faced. 'Its force had not abated,' it was said. The observation that 'the Rangers meant business' put the prospect of an Ayr win in even more jeopardy. Reid shot against the post with the Ayr goal yawning open in front of him. Spoiling tactics had to be resorted to in order to curb the attacking enthusiasm of Rangers, although, in a breakaway, Joe Cassidy beat Kelso then crossed for Jacky Goodwin, who shot too high with what should have been a simple chance. Back came Rangers. In one spell of pressure, they won four corner-kicks, one after another. Once again, Ayr United broke clear for Jimmy Richardson to cross for Alec Gray, who contrived to miss an open goal from ten yards. Another chance to put the game out of reach had been scorned!

Rangers 1	Ayr United 3
Reid	*Richardson (2),*
	J.L. Goodwin

Top left, Willie McStay;
top right, Switcher McLaughlan;
centre, Herbert Dainty;
bottom right, Jimmy Richardson.

It was a potentially costly miss in light of the Rangers goal that followed. Anderson crossed from the left and Reid turned swiftly prior to scoring with a well-executed shot.

In response, Ayr United attacked and forced a corner-kick, which was taken by Alec Gray. The ball floated nicely in the direction of Jimmy Richardson, who headed past Herbert Lock to make it 3-1. 'There was much handshaking at this result and Richardson was magnaminous enough to give Gray a handshake for his perfectly placed ball,' it was reported.

Still Rangers refused to concede defeat. They responded by attacking aggressively. Too aggressively! Ayr goalkeeper Jack Lyall was punched and hacked whilst in possession of the ball. In 1915, such behaviour did not even constitute an offence. In fact, Lyall was even blamed for the scene because it was considered that there was no need for him to hold on to the ball for so long. An injury to John Bell caused him to be taken off, but soon afterwards the final whistle sounded.

Rangers: Lock, Kelso, Craig, Gordon, Pursell, Baird, Paterson, Bowie, Reid, Cairns and Anderson.
Ayr United: Lyall, Bell, McStay. A.H. Goodwin, Dainty, McLaughlan, Middleton, J.L. Goodwin, Richardson, Cassidy and Gray.

Ayr United v. Kilmarnock

20 September 1919
Somerset Park

Scottish League First Division

To put this result into context, it should be understood that Kilmarnock proceeded to win the Scottish Cup in season 1919/20, whilst three days earlier Albion Rovers, destined for the final, had lost 4-0 at Somerset Park. The derby score-line amply illustrated the type of spectacle witnessed but, prior to the kick-off, it appeared that the proceedings would be spoiled by the strong wind that blew across the pitch. In addition, there was a strong sun to contend with.

In the summer of 1919, James MacDonald, the Kilmarnock manager, had switched allegiance to Ayr United. This may have given some kind of tactical advantage. The idea that olden-day football was devoid of tactical awareness is one of those perpetual myths. As early as the turn of the twentieth century, Ayr FC had employed an offside trap.

From the kick-off, the game settled into a pattern of predictably even exchanges. It was a pattern which threatened to be broken when Billy Crosbie broke clear and found himself in a situation from which a pass to Jock Smith would have brought an almost certain goal. The pass was not forthcoming, however, and Crosbie elected to shoot from his less favourable position and put the ball behind. Billy Crosbie was again prominent when embarking on a run which culminated in a cross. When the ball came over, Jock Smith and Jimmy Richardson seemed to divert the attention of goalkeeper Tom Blair. Switcher McLaughlan was then able to attempt a shot, which Blair got his hands to but could not prevent from crossing the line. The goal time was thirty-three minutes.

The lead was almost increased when a shot from Jimmy Richardson was saved magnificently by Blair. Both players were applauded for this incident. Yet, in the case of Richardson, even more generous applause was to come his way after forty-two minutes. He succeeded in beating both of the Kilmarnock full-backs before crashing the ball into the net.

Suitably buoyant, the second half saw Ayr United attack briskly. Neil McBain netted with a header but he was ruled offside in a disputed decision. The third goal remained elusive when a fierce shot from Johnny Crosbie 'soiled the paint on the crossbar'. McBain resumed on the offensive with a fine run on goal and was most unfortunate not to score, but the ball broke to Jock Smith who made it 3-0 with fifty-four minutes played. It had not yet been discovered that Neil McBain's best position was centre-half rather than inside forward. Nor had it been discovered that Jock Smith was more suited to playing at full-back rather than on the left wing.

Merely two minutes elapsed before the next scoring action. That was when Billy Crosbie put the game beyond all reasonable doubt with an angular drive. At 4-0 down, Killie showed commendable character with a renewed commitment which put the home defence through some testing moments. Alex Gillespie, at the heart of that defence, cleared four successive attacks. Gradually, the flow of the game was reversed and Ayr United resumed the ascendancy. Regarding this stage of the match, it is on record that they 'began to toy with the opposition'. There was even a moment of humour, unwittingly instigated by the referee, who restarted the game with a bounce-up after Johnny Crosbie had been fouled. Johnny Crosbie then broke through and, with only the goalkeeper to beat, shot against a post. Soon afterwards, Jock Smith went close with an overhead kick. A further attack involved Jock Smith passing to Johnny Crosbie, who shot too high with Tom Blair at his mercy. Just when it seemed that he was destined not to score, Johnny Crosbie succeeded in shooting past Blair

Ayr United 5
McLaughlan, Richardson, Smith
W. Crosbie, J. Crosbie

Kilmarnock 0

It was difficult to keep larger clubs at bay. Neil McBain (left) and Johnny Crosbie are seen here in the colours of Manchester United and Birmingham City respsectively.

from a corner-kick. The ball glanced off Jock Smith's leg on the way in, but it was not diverted sufficiently for the Beith farmer to be credited with the goal. With three minutes remaining, the score-line was highly satisfactory at 5-0.

Observant readers will have noticed that there were two Crosbies amongst the scorers. Johnny and Billy were cousins who were natives of that famous footballing nursery, the Ayrshire mining village of Glenbuck. Billy Crosbie was purchased from Vale of Clyde for the less-than-princely sum of £7. It seems curious to relate that this transaction in the Ayr United account book was dated two days later than the Kilmarnock match.

Look at the Ayr United team listed below and you will see the names of six full internationals, five of whom appeared for Scotland whilst still attached to the club. The names are Phil McCloy, Jimmy Hogg, Johnny Crosbie, Jimmy Richardson, Neil McBain and Jock Smith. Whenever international honours are listed, Jimmy Richardson's name is almost always omitted since his appearances were made in 'Victory' internationals. These matches were deemed to be unofficial, but he shed sweat for his country and this is worthy of acknowledgement.

Ayr United: Kerr, Semple, McCloy, Hogg, Gillespie, McLaughlan, W.Crosbie, J.Crosbie, Richardson, McBain and Smith.

Kilmarnock: Blair, Hamilton, Gibson, Shortt, Neave, Mackie, Bagan, Higgins, McLean, McHallum and McPhail.

CELTIC v. AYR UNITED

11 November 1922
Celtic Park

Scottish League First Division

The gentlemen of the press were unanimous in the belief that Ayr United would lose this match. An Ayr win at Celtic Park was without historical precedent and, apart from blind optimism, there was no reason to suppose that the trend would be broken.

Celtic pressed immediately into attack. Phil McCloy and George Nisbet blocked early efforts but Celtic continued to pile forward with attacking abandon. Especially close was Adam McLean, who struck Nisbet's crossbar with a shot. When the visitors did manage to breach home territory, Murdoch McKenzie shot behind, prior to Patsy Gallacher doing the same at the Ayr end. Again, a counter attack was launched. Jamie McLean crossed in the direction of Tommy Kilpatrick, who returned the ball in the direction from which it had come. It then landed nicely for Murdoch McKenzie, who blasted it past goalkeeper John Hughes. The joy of this goal was tempered by the knowledge that just six minutes had elapsed. It would be inaccurate to state that this silenced the home crowd. The attendance was variously estimated at five, six and seven thousand – a sparse assembly in the vast bowl that comprised Celtic Park. To put it more succinctly, that crowd could not have been unduly intimidating anyway. Celtic historians have acknowledged that, in this particular era, their club could rely on a vast support but only when the occasion was big enough. Alas, the visit of Ayr United did not have the allure of an Old Firm derby or a cup final.

After Jimmy McLeod had conceded a free-kick for handling, Phil McCloy joined George Nisbet in the Ayr goal in a determined attempt to defend the set-piece. Willie McStay took the kick 'with great strength'. One journalist described what happened next in the following terms. 'How Nisbet succeeded in getting his hands on the ball so quickly we do not know, but he did, and in trying to assist him, McCloy was injured.'

Celtic's ascendancy receded to the extent that Ayr United nearly scored again. Donald Slade released Tommy Kilpatrick, who struck a shot that was only partially saved by Hughes. It took the intervention of home full-back Willie Cringan to prevent the ball from crossing the line. When the flow of play again favoured Celtic, they were let down by their lack of marksmanship. Willie McStay was off-target with a free-kick, and then similar luck befell an attempt from Patsy Gallacher. A penalty claim brought a fleeting moment of panic. The ball had struck a hand after being driven into the Ayr box, but there was no intent, therefore referee Peter Craigmyle correctly adjudged that there was no substance to the claim. At the opposite end, the Ayr players then had cause for complaint when an offside decision was disputed.

Would it be possible to protect the slender lead in the second half? It transpired that the lead was cancelled out just one minute into what was then sometimes poetically referred to as 'the concluding moiety'. George Nisbet threw the ball over the heads of his colleague Jock Smith and Celtic's Adam McLean. It then bounced up and struck Smith on the arm. A penalty kick was awarded. During a loan spell, Willie McStay had rendered three-and-a-half years of fine service to Ayr United, but here, in 1922, he did his duty by converting the penalty kick into a goal.

At 1-1, it would no doubt have been imagined that a Celtic fight-back was only just beginning. A fight-back was indeed about to materialise, yet it would not favour Celtic. Jimmy Hogg was not reputed for subtle creativity. He was a tough-tackling half-back, who preferred the robust approach. Ambitiously, he embarked on a solo run and beat three men

Celtic 1
W. McStay

Ayr United 4
McKenzie (2),
Hogg, Slade

League Goals 1922/23	
McKenzie	13
John McLean	8
Cunningham	7
Slade	5
Howard	3
McCloy	2
Quinn	2
Hogg	1
Kilpatrick	1
James McLean	1
Total	**43**

Phil McCloy.

in succession before driving the ball into the net. An incident followed in which Willie Cringan (a former Ayr United player) passed back to John Hughes (a future Ayr United goal-keeper), who struggled to gain possession and had to watch the ball roll out for a corner-kick. From that corner-kick, a Willie Gibson header was put over by Hughes for another flag-kick. When next the ball came over, Murdoch McKenzie struck the crossbar with a header. McKenzie had further cause to curse his luck when he netted from a Fred Howard cross. A seemingly fine goal was disallowed.

A tactical manoeuvre involved Celtic's centre forward, Adam McLean, swapping positions with outside-left, Jean McFarlane. However, Celtic's attempts to draw level were fruitless. Jamie McLean missed from close range, although a further Ayr goal was barely delayed. A Murdoch McKenzie drive stretched the lead to 3-1 with seven minutes left. Just three minutes remained when Donald Slade concluded the scoring with a long-range left-foot drive. Prior to the end, Fred Howard appeared to be on the point of stretching the score to 5-1. He was frustrated by an offside decision which was described as 'glaringly wrong'.

Match referee Peter Craigmyle took charge of Ayr United matches as late as 1949 (his final spell coming during the club's Highland tour in that year).

Celtic: Hughes, Cringan, Murphy, Gilchrist, W. McStay, J. McStay, Connolly, Gallacher, McLean, Thomson and McFarlane.
Ayr United: Nisbet, Smith, McCloy, Hogg, McLeod, Gibson, Kilpatrick, Slade, Howard, McKenzie and McLean.

AYR UNITED v. RANGERS

27 January 1923
Somerset Park

Scottish Cup Second Round
Attendance: 15,853

This was a time in which it was still permissible for a club to buy ground rights in the Scottish Cup. In the previous round, Ayr United had offered Arbroath Athletic (a different club from Arbroath) a cash inducement to shift the tie to Somerset Park from their own Hospital Park. Arbroath Athletic were amenable to the idea, but only at a price of £300. The Ayr United board disagreed with the fee, not that it mattered in the end. The team simply went to Arbroath and enjoyed a leisurely 3-0 win. Then, when drawn at home to Rangers, a financial inducement was made to switch the tie to Ibrox Park. The money was refused.

1923 was a Golden Jubilee year for Rangers, and they no doubt considered it a special year in which to pursue a League and Scottish Cup double. As regards the latter, an obstacle to their ambition was an Ayr United team that included ten players who had been recruited from junior football. The sole exception was Tommy Kilpatrick, formerly of Hibs and Dundee. Somewhat parochially, it can also be stated that the scorers in this tie were both Ayr natives and products of the Schools Football League. Jamie McLean was also an Ayr man whilst Smith, Hogg, McLeod and Cunningham were Ayrshiremen, though not of Ayr itself.

The crowd figure was a record attendance for Somerset Park at the time, despite people staying away for fear that they would not get in. There was also the counter attraction of a Kilmarnock v. East Fife tie at Rugby Park.

Ayr United came out first, with captain Willie Gibson at the head of the line. The players then trotted onto a pitch that was in traditionally fine condition, despite the previous rain. Everything seemed to be conducive to a decent tie and it was especially heartening that Ayr United had wind advantage in the first half. Then, in the opening minutes, the tie came to an undignified halt. The ball burst! It had landed on the spikes which topped one of the walls around Somerset Park.

Early pressure was exerted on the Rangers goal. Following a corner-kick, there was an appeal for a penalty. It was claimed that Dixon, the visiting centre-half, had handled. The claim was an ambitious one. Still the home side piled forward. Harry Cunningham missed with a header and a further attack was broken up by a fine save from Robb. Yet again, Rangers territory was invaded, and Willie Gibson was brought down inside the box. This may have been a better claim than the one before, but the result was the same.

The Ayr goal was threatened in an attacking move in which Henderson, the visiting centre forward, cutely handled the ball. It was done so subtly as to escape the attention of Mr Bell, the referee. Justice was done when the ball went behind for a goal-kick.

At the start of the match, the 'Honest Men' appeared to be motivated by eagerness. This gradually gave way to a confidence, which manifested itself in yet more attacking moves. Tommy Kilpatrick shot dangerously across the face of the Rangers goal, only to see the ball clear the post. In a further close scrape at that end, Manderson managed to block the ball on the line before his goalkeeper pounced on it. Back came Ayr United for a raid in which John McLean failed to punish hesitancy on the part of Manderson. Harry Cunningham then asserted himself by forcing two fruitless corners. Archibald did manage to stage a breakaway for Rangers, but he was beaten by the speed of Willie Gibson, who averted a potentially dangerous situation by getting the ball into touch.

In the second half, Ayr United resumed the ascendancy. John McLean and Murdoch McKenzie converged on a loose ball. The Ayr men were beaten to it by the Rangers goal-

Ayr United 2

McKenzie,
McLean (John)

Rangers 0

Scottish Cup Goals 1922/23	
McKenzie	2
Cunningham	1
John McLean	2
Total	**5**

Willie Gibson.

keeper, but it was a close thing, and the latter got hurt for his efforts. Another player to pick up an injury was Ayr's Murdoch McKenzie. He was concussed after inadvertently getting his head in the way of a drive from team-mate Jimmy McLeod! The attacking momentum continued to roll yet the superiority still would not convert itself into a goal. Again, a penalty claim was made. This time the incident involved a Harry Cunningham drive, which was stopped by the hand of a Rangers defender. Again, the claim went unheeded.

With nineteen minutes left, the Rangers goal was breached at last. McCandless failed to clear a Tommy Kilpatrick cross and Murdoch McKenzie took the opportunity to fire the ball high into the net. The shock of the goal stung Rangers into attack and they quickly forced two corner-kicks. Then the home team broke in a move that saw John McLean pass to Tommy Kilpatrick, who returned it for John McLean to deftly slip the ball into the net. This happened just two minutes after the opening goal. Faced with a 2-0 deficit and seventeen minutes in which to attempt to retrieve the situation, Rangers became desperate. Dangerously desperate! Despite this, the last chance of the match fell to Jamie McLean who burst through only to miss the target.

In the aftermath of a fine result, trainer James Quaite was praised on the grounds that 'stamina and fitness played a prominent part in the victory'. Unfortunately, Ayr went on to suffer a third-round elimination, losing 2-0 away to Third Lanark.

Ayr United: Nisbet, Smith, McCloy, Hogg, McLeod, Gibson, Kilpatrick, Cunningham, John McLean, McKenzie and Jamie McLean.
Rangers: Robb, Manderson, McCandless, Meiklejohn, Dixon, Muirhead, Archibald, Cunningham, Henderson, Cairns and Morton.

AIRDRIE v. AYR UNITED

8 March 1924   Scottish Cup Quarter-Final
Broomfield Park

In time-honoured fashion, it is commonplace for supporters to moan about grievances, whether actual or perceived. On 8 March 1924, Ayr United were the victims of a gross injustice, which still had supporters complaining about it more than half a century later. The festering resentment was the reaction to the conclusion of this Scottish Cup tie. Trains descending on Airdrie from Glasgow were heavily laden, and it was estimated that as many as 23,000 were in the ground when the game kicked off, several minutes late, at 3.34 p.m. Those who straggled in just several minutes after the kick-off missed the opening goal.

Murdoch McKenzie was fouled near the penalty box and Kirkwood, on loan from Rangers, hit the free-kick in the direction of Tommy Kilpatrick, who crossed for John McLean to hit a first-time drive, which goalkeeper Ewart failed to hold. John Anderson was then left with the easy task of touching the ball home from point-blank range. Just two minutes had been played and there was now a distinct possibility that Ayr United would reach the Scottish Cup semi-final for the first time. Of course, the time factor was a major concern and, surely enough, Airdrie began to lay siege to the Ayr United goal. The persistence of this pressure proved too much when, in the twenty-second minute, Hughie Gallacher, still on the threshold of fame, hooked the ball over his head and past George Nisbet in the Ayr goal. Nisbet had been beaten by the unexpectedness of Gallacher's attempt.

The levelling goal inspired Airdrie yet further, and they won corner after corner. Nisbet proved to be in fine form and, in front of him, his fellow defenders were supplemented by forwards who had been pulled back out of necessity. Not only corners were conceded. The strength of the tackling also caused free-kicks to be conceded. The closing stages of the first half were described in the following terms. 'Half-time was getting near with Airdrie still dancing around Ayr's citadel, and when lemon time did come it found the scores still one each.'

In the years ahead, Hughie Gallacher was to forge a reputation as a moody genius and this tie saw him display both of his main character traits. He was let off after deliberately aiming a kick at Kirkwood. Later, following a free-kick, he headed over the Ayr crossbar. Gallacher again broke through, only to be beaten by Nisbet, who averted the considerable danger by diverting the ball away with his leg.

Outside-right Tommy Kilpatrick easily had the better of Airdrie left-back McQueen, and he succeeded in getting in a cross, which was met by John McLean, who drove the ball against the crossbar. The rebound then fell for Harry Cunningham, who struck a shot that found the net but was disallowed for an offside award. Ayr United continued to attack, then Airdrie retaliated strongly. A Howieson strike hit the Ayr crossbar, but this incident was almost minor in comparison with the game's finale. The tale of what happened in the last minute was passed on for posterity.

A John McLean shot went wide and, when the goalkeeper picked the ball up, it had already crossed the line. However, he kicked it back into play and Mr Humphrey, the referee, allowed the game to continue rather than insist on a goal-kick. McLean got possession again and centred to John Anderson, who connected with a first-time shot that thundered into the net. This was a sensational development as the final whistle was just about due. The referee signalled the goal and, at this point, the Airdrie directors were seen to vacate their seats in order to make their way towards the boardroom. The Ayr players lined up for the re-centre

Airdrie 1   **Ayr United 1**
Gallacher   *Anderson*

Scottish Cup Goals 1923/24	
Cunningham	4
McKenzie	2
Anderson	3
Total	9

Harry Cunningham.

and watched on, while the Airdrie players shamelessly surrounded the referee in protest about something which was unapparent. As a result of those protests, the weak-willed Mr Humphrey consulted both linesmen in turn and then disallowed the goal. Yes, a ball had been kicked from hand when a goal-kick should have been given, but that had been an advantage to the home side, besides which the referee had been aware of what had happened and had allowed the game to proceed. Some reports suggested that a totally unjustified offside award against McLean had formed the basis of the decision. In either event, it was a major sickener and a total travesty and there were fans, then young, who were still speaking about it in their old age.

At Somerset Park, even extra time failed to produce a goal in the replay. The second replay, at Ibrox Park, was drawn 1-1, again after extra time. On the day after that match, the third replay took place, again at Ibrox Park. Hughie Gallacher scored the only goal of the match on that occasion, and it was of little consolation that Airdrie went on to lift the Scottish Cup in 1924. That they proceeded beyond the last eight was down to a weak and erroneous refereeing decision.

Ayr United eventually did reach the semi-final stage of the Scottish Cup but the wait to do so lasted until 1973.

Airdrie: Ewart, Dick, McQueen, Preston, McDougall, Bennie, Reid, Russell, Gallacher, Howieson and Somerville.

Ayr United: Nisbet, Smith, McCloy, Hogg, Kirkwood, Murphy, Kilpatrick, Cunningham, Anderson, McKenzie and John McLean.

Ayr United v. Dundee United

14 April 1928   Scottish League Second Division
Somerset Park

The 1927/28 season saw Ayr United romp to the Second Division championship, and it was further marked by Jimmy Smith scoring sixty-six League goals for the club. His four goals in this match took him to number sixty-five. To put the result into context, it is worth commenting that a Dundee United win would have elevated them to second position. Yet typical post-match comments included: 'The play was too one-sided to permit of any serious comment' and 'The Northerners were made to look very foolish at times'.

The dubious lure of an Old Firm Scottish Cup final attracted many fans away from this area. They missed a performance that caused Ayr United to be described as 'super excellent'. It was an accurate assessment when it is considered that a 6-1 half-time lead was achieved while playing against the wind.

Right at the start, Jimmy Smith suffered a bad kick, which caused him to require treatment. The assault was swiftly avenged when Danny Tolland headed home a Jim Nisbet corner-kick with just two minutes played. When Jocky Simpson hit a perfect pass for Jimmy Smith to run on and make it 2-0, there were only eleven minutes on the clock.

From this point on, attacks on the Dundee United goal were unrelenting. Only a corner-kick was given after a tackle in which Smith was badly fouled inside the penalty area. Nisbet became the next home player to suffer from a cynical tackle, and it resulted in a free-kick which was taken by 'Wullie' Robertson. From this set-piece, Smith was picked out and, in turn, Simpson was fed with the ball. The latter hit a scoring shot with twenty-four minutes played.

Dundee United then became aggressive, not with yet more wayward tackling, but in the attacking sense. Hutchison headed narrowly over, then Walker shot narrowly past. It was the prelude to Bain scoring for the visitors with a long-range shot. It was almost pegged back to 3-2, when a free-kick gave goalkeeper Bob Hepburn a lot of concern and he was fouled whilst averting the danger. A free-kick relieved the pressure, and that was as hectic as things were to get for Hepburn.

Jimmy Smith chased the visiting goalkeeper for a loose ball. The 'keeper got to it first, but the ball came off him to leave Smith with an empty net to shoot at. It was an easy goal (scored on thirty-nine minutes). Three minutes later, Billy Brae scored from a free-kick, taken from near the corner flag. Time remained for yet another first-half goal. Left-back Dorward tripped Nisbet at the expense of a penalty, which Smith converted. 6-1 ahead at the interval and awaiting the wind advantage in the second half! It is difficult to conceive of a more satisfactory situation.

Danny Tolland set up Smith for the goal which made it 7-1 with forty minutes left. With his personal haul standing at four goals, he shaved the crossbar with a free-kick and then headed over from a Nisbet cross. Tolland also had an opportunity, but he preferred to indulge in what was described as 'sand dancing'. Another foul inside the box should have brought another penalty, but it was not given. Shortly afterwards, a net-bound shot from Smith struck right-back Taylor on the leg and was diverted to safety. With the goalkeeper posted missing, this was especially bad luck.

The opportunity to pursue a record score presented itself. It was a wasted opportunity as the Ayr United team preferred to indulge in 'fancy trickery' during most of the second half. To begin with, the spectators were amused but, when the novelty wore off, many of them

---

Ayr United 7   **Dundee United 1**
Tolland, Smith (4),   *Bain*
Simpson, Brae

From left to right: Tommy Kilpatrick (absent against Dundee United), Danny Tolland and Jimmy Smith.

were seen to leave the ground before the end. Danny Tolland in particular had a reputation of being an outstanding ball-player, and this game afforded him the irresistible chance to show off his repertoire of skills. At times, it bordered on farce.

The Dundee United team did not remotely possess the skill of the home side. They were, on average, heavier, and they showed visibly their displeasure at such a humiliation. This displeasure manifested itself in foul play with, not surprisingly, Jimmy Smith bearing the brunt of it. His immediate adversary, centre-half Walker, injured himself and had to be helped off the field after a failed assault on the Ayr marksman.

It was the third occasion that Smith scored four goals in a League match that season, while on two occasions he bagged five. His six League hat-tricks of 1927/28 were almost routine by comparison.

Ayr United: Hepburn, Purdon, Fleming, Robertson, McColgan, Turnbull, Nisbet, Tolland, Smith, Simpson and Brae.

Dundee United: Johnstone, Taylor, Dorward, Jock Kay, Walker, Bain, 'Newman', Hart, Hutchison, Campbell and J.S. Kay.

Partick Thistle v. Ayr United

10 November 1928   Scottish League First Division
Firhill Park

The unexpectedness of what lay ahead was beautifully expressed by a journalist who covered the match. 'When we boarded a Maryhill tramcar at West Nile Street, Glasgow, on Saturday afternoon, we little knew what a fine football feast was in store for us at Firhill Park. The day was damp and, after the dampening effect of the second half of the previous Saturday's game at Somerset Park, Ayr people's enthusiasm was not very great. The abnormally heavy rain of the day had rendered the playing pitch an absolute quagmire. About the time for starting, the sun discovered a crack in the clouds through which it had cast its cheery beams on the glittering ground surface, but it didn't remain with us long.'

The mention of the week before referred to a match in which Ayr United had led Aberdeen 3-0 only for the result to finish as a 3-3 draw. This week, there was to be no semblance of a second-half fadeout. To understand the relevance of this 8-4 win, it should be understood that Partick Thistle held a 4-2 half-time lead.

Early pressure put the Ayr goal under immediate threat. In the seesaw nature of the game, Ayr United did manage some counter-attacks before the home side regained the ascendancy. Outside-right Ness was an especially troublesome opponent and, when he shot into a ruck of players, Ayr United full-back Norman Price contrived to head the ball into his own net.

In an attempt to redress the situation, Jimmy Smith was unlucky with two good headers. During this spell of pressure, Jimmy Nisbet had a shot put out for a corner by goalkeeper Jackson. From that corner, Billy Brae nearly scored, but Jackson diverted the attempt for a further corner, which Brae again nearly scored from. Partick then broke upfield and, with twenty minutes played, J. McLeod made it 2-0. It is often said that a team is vulnerable when they have just scored and, one minute later, Jimmy Smith scored with a header which was described as remarkable. After a further minute had elapsed, Simpson made it 3-1 for Partick Thistle. Yet again, there was a gap of just a minute until the next goal. Nisbet connected with a drive that Jackson got his fingertips to, but could not hold – the score was now 3-2. Three goals in as many minutes! The match did die down a little after this, although Ayr United's deficit was extended to 4-2 before half-time. Bob Hepburn had the ball in his hands, but this did not prevent him from being dispossessed by Ballantyne to allow Ness the chance to score. All perfectly legal in 1928!

Had Ayr United gone 5-2 behind, it is questionable whether the impetus for a fight-back would have been there. The reason for raising the point is that the home outside-left (Simpson) had a point-blank shot on the Ayr goal, which Hepburn saved with his face. The value of that save was emphasised when Willie Neil passed to Jimmy Smith, who ran on to fire past Jackson with ten minutes of the second half played. Nine minutes later, Smith was the provider for Billy Brae to make it 4-4 with a great shot. In the very next minute, Ayr United sensationally took a 5-4 lead when the fabulous Smith evaded a strong tackle from Paton and drove the ball past the beleaguered Jackson. The lead was now held by Ayr for the first time, and the players were in no mood to relinquish it.

From this point on, the attacks on the Thistle goal became constant. A free-kick on the edge of the penalty area was met by Danny Tolland, who headed the ball in the direction of Smith, who fired it into the net. Fifteen minutes remained. Nisbet crossed for Smith to hammer in his fifth goal of the match and Ayr United's seventh. Eleven minutes were now left. When Turnbull shot Ayr United 8-4 ahead, six minutes remained, but this goal concluded

---

Partick Thistle 4
Price (og), J. McLeod, Simpson, Ness

Ayr United 8
Smith (5), Nisbet, Brae, Turnbull

League Goals 1928/29	
Smith	26
Brae	11
Nisbet	6
Neil	4
Tolland	4
McCall	3
Riley	3
Robertson	3
Simpson	2
Fleming	1
Turnbull	1
Wardrope	1
Total	**65**

Billy Brae.

the considerable scoring. It remains a club record for away goals in a League fixture. A magnificent save from Hepburn prevented a further Thistle goal in the closing minutes. An injury to Danny Tolland prevented him from finishing the match, although he did manage to scrape the crossbar with a shot before retiring from the action. Had either, or both, of those chances gone in, the score-line would have looked even more staggering.

On 28 September 1957, a Second Division fixture ended Ayr United 7 Forfar Athletic 4, but the second-half heroics at Firhill Park in November 1928 were beyond comparison.

The last words on it will be left to the poetic scribe referred to in the opening paragraph. 'Forward, the great man was Smith who, we think, played his best game for Ayr United. He was the hero of the play'.

Partick Thistle: Jackson, O'Hare, Paton, Richmond, Lambie, E. McLeod, Ness, J. McLeod, Ballantyne, Fraser and Simpson.

Ayr United: Hepburn, Price, Fleming, Neil, Robertson, Turnbull, Nisbet, Tolland, Smith, Simpson and Brae.

AYR UNITED v. HAMILTON ACCIES

29 March 1930   Scottish League First Division
Somerset Park

At first glance a draw at home to Hamilton Accies may not fit the profile of a 'classic match'. This was a season in which Ayr United finished ninth in the First Division table, and the Accies ended up more modestly placed at thirteenth in the twenty-club League. Hamilton did have a good Scottish Cup run, which had culminated in a semi-final defeat against Partick Thistle, the week before this game at Ayr. Yet, beforehand, there was nothing to suggest that the fixture would produce anything out of the ordinary. In fact, for eighty-seven minutes, the match, from the Ayr United viewpoint, was palpably not a classic.

An interesting novelty was that this match coincided with Students' Day. A student with a blacked-out face stood in attendance at the toss-up and, on the conclusion of this pre-match ritual, he hastily grabbed the referee's penny as a contribution towards charitable causes.

Of more concern was the serious business of football. The Accies pressed straight into attack, and left-back John McBain had to clear the danger twice during this spell. Once the pressure had been relieved, Billy Brae almost put Ayr United in front when goalkeeper Nicoll had difficulty in holding his shot. It was surely a matter of gratitude to the custodian that nothing worse than a corner-kick was conceded. Suitably encouraged, the offensive was maintained and the visiting defence became taxed to straining point. Again the pendulum swung and the onus was on McBain to effect another of his clearances. Alas, the relief was only momentary, and Bob Hepburn had to pull off a brilliant save from Moffat. A McMenemy shot narrowly cleared the Ayr crossbar, and two further shots were blocked by the Ayr defence. Hamilton came close to being punished for an inability to make their pressure count. J. Wilson (one of three Wilsons in the Hamilton team) cleared the ball from under the crossbar, and a further raid saw Robert Hart go close with a header. Assaults on the Hamilton goal persisted. The goalkeeper finished up on his knees to save from Pearson Ferguson.

With twenty-five minutes played, the stalemate was broken when Wilson broke clear to fire the Accies in front. Either D. Wilson or F. Wilson scored the goal, but it is impossible to be precise since there were conflicting reports. Three minutes later, Andy McCall headed an equaliser.

In what remained of the first half, Danny Tolland shot just inches too high and Nicoll had difficulty in saving from Billy Brae. At the other end, a good chance fell to D. Wilson, but he was thwarted by the speed of John McBain.

At half-time, the students reappeared. They were described as 'gaily bedecked'. The crowd was entertained by their antics, but it was soon obvious that 'they were not giving the entertainment for nothing'. They were there to collect money!

At the start of the second half, it was not long before the Ayr goal was visited. 'By the exercise of a supreme effort', Bob Hepburn saved a low shot from King. Pressure had to be sustained for several minutes but, once the brunt of those attacks had been borne, Tolland and McLeod brought out saves from Nicoll. Then came a raid on Ayr teritory from which King put the visitors 2-1 in front. The damage was almost compounded when Jimmy McLeod contrived to mis-kick the ball over his own crossbar. However, this was merely a stay of execution. D. Wilson succeeded in making it 3-1 after a wonderful solo effort. There were no conflicting reports about which of the Wilson clan scored this one. The Accies threatened to take the score to seemingly insurmountable proportions. A shot from King beat Hepburn

---

Ayr United 3
McCall, Nisbet,
Brae

Hamilton Accies 3
D. Wilson/F. Wilson (conflicting reports),
King, D. Wilson

Ayr United FC 1929/30. On the far left, with the glasses, is trainer Jimmy Dalziel. On the far right is secretary-manager Archie Buchanan. Tommy Robertson is second from the right in the back row and the goalkeeper third from the left in the back row is Bob Hepburn. From left to right, middle row: -?-,Turnbull, McLeod, McCall. Front row: Nisbet, Tolland, Fleming, Brae, -?-.

before hitting one post followed by the other, eventually rebounding into play. This was a major slice of luck for Ayr United.

Pearson Ferguson had a good chance to reduce the arrears. He found himself in a good shooting position, but unselfishly elected to pass to Robert Hart. It would have been better if he had chosen the selfish option. Nicoll emerged from his goal to gain possession before Hart had the opportunity to shoot.

With three minutes to go, and the majority of spectators no doubt contemplating making their way to the exits, Jimmy Nisbet managed to shoot high into the net from an awkward angle. Desperation then crept into the play of the home team. In adopting a policy of attacking abandon, there was nothing to lose. Danny Tolland spearheaded a raid which ended in Billy Brae making it 3-3 with a strong shot. Not content with this, a further raid was launched and Andy McCall struck a shot that was heading for the back of the Hamilton net. It did not arrive at the intended destination due to the ball being blocked by a defender. It could so easily have been three goals in the last three minutes – still, the closing minutes were sensational enough.

It was observed that spectators had left several minutes early when Ayr United still trailed 3-1. This may have been attributable to the rain, but it is more likely that they considered the game to be lost.

Ayr United: Hepburn, Fleming, McBain, Turnbull, McLeod, McCall, Nisbet, Tolland, Hart, Brae and Ferguson.

Hamilton Accies: Nicoll, Allan, J. Wilson, McDougall, Watson, Bulloch, F. Wilson, Moffat, D. Wilson, McMenemy and King.

Ayr United v. Clackmannan

17 January 1931   Scottish Cup First Round
Somerset Park   Attendance: 4,296

This was a bad day for a lot of small clubs who were seeking to negotiate a way through to the second round of the Scottish Cup. Dundee United beat Sanquhar-based Nithsdale Wanderers 14-0 to establish what remains a club-record score. Partick Thistle enjoyed a 16-0 rout against Larkhall-based Royal Albert and that too remains a club-record score. Dundee beat Fraserburgh 10-1 to establish a club record, which was eventually eclipsed in March 1947 when, remarkably, they won 10-0 twice. Back on that mad day in January 1931, Hearts eliminated Stenhousemuir 9-1, while Arbroath, Rangers, Clyde, Kilmarnock and King's Park all scored seven. Six clubs also succeeded in scoring six. The result shown below was considered to be a club-record score at the time, but it was a wrongful claim since Whithorn had fallen by a larger margin, 10-0, at Somerset Park in a Scottish Cup qualifying tie on 16 September 1911. (Elsewhere in this book wins of 10-1 and 11-1 are also covered.)

One of the reports on this tie contained comments that were patronising in the extreme: 'The game was in many respects farcical but the visitors played up manfully and showed a determination and gallantry which spoke well of them'. In truth, they played up so manfully that they were 8-1 down at half-time.

Ayr United had a strong wind in their favour in the first half and visiting goalkeeper Shepherd saved well from Billy Brae, Pearson Ferguson and Danny Tolland. Yet, when the opening goal went in, merely a few minutes had been played. The strike was credited to Tolland but the ball deflected off a defender en route. Pearson Ferguson found the net with an angled shot and had a goal disallowed just afterwards for an infringement. Tolland made it 3-0 with a neat drive, then Pearson Ferguson got another.

The team from the 'Wee Coonty' eventually made so bold as to force Fleming to concede a corner-kick. At least, that was what the referee indicated, but a posse of visiting players complained and the official decided to consult a linesman. After that confab he changed his award to a penalty kick. Hepburn initially saved Reid's attempt from the spot but he only diverted the ball against the crossbar. This allowed Reid to take the chance to net the rebound.

The well worn route to Shepherd's goal was immediately retraced and Charlie McGillivray made the score 5-1. The Ayr forwards came back for more and Pearson Ferguson was fouled for a clear penalty award. What happened next was described as an 'extraordinary spectacle'. Bob Hepburn exercised his right as captain to select himself to take the penalty. When goalkeeper faced goalkeeper the ball was deposited into the back of the net with a left-foot shot. Charlie McGillivray scored twice more before the interval. 8-1 at the break! The loss of wind advantage was an irrelevance.

What was said to the visitors at half-time can only be guessed at, but they must have been told something on the have-a-go theme. This view is borne out by the fact that they came back out and started launching into attack. The strategy was justified when some determined pressure culminated in a goal from Wright. However they were unable to maintain the offensive for a sustained spell. Billy Brae wormed his way through the Clackmannan defence to make it 9-2. A long range shot from Danny Tolland took Ayr's total into double figures and McGillivray topped it off near the end.

A summary of this tie included an interesting philosophy: 'Clackmannan did what they could not exceed – their best'. It was just too bad that their best was not very good. Further

---

Ayr United 11   **Clackmannan 2**
  Tolland (3), Ferguson (2), McGillivray (4),   *Reid, Wright*
  Hepburn, Brae

Most Scottish Cup goals in a match		
4	Charlie McGillivray v. Clackmannan	17/01/31
4	Bobby Stevenson v. Berwick Rangers	04/02/56
3	A.L. Muir v. Lochgelly United	01/02/22
3	Alex Sharp v. Berwick Rangers	19/01/29
3	Danny Tolland v. Clackmannan	17/01/31
3	Jimmy Baker v. Queen's Park	10/02/51
3	Peter Price v. Airdrie	27/02/60
3	Davie McCulloch v. Stranraer	16/02/74
3	George McLean v. Stranraer	16/02/74
3	Ian Ferguson v. Alloa Athletic	24/01/98

In the year of publication these are the only instances of Ayr United players scoring three or more in a Scottish Cup tie.

Bob Hepburn.

comments called it 'a slaughter of the innocents' and mentioned that the opposition 'were in no way a match for players who are competing with the best in the country every Saturday'.

Although not a club record in terms of winning margins, it was a club record in terms of goals scored in a competitive fixture. On an individual basis, Charlie McGillivray became the first Ayr United player to score four goals in a Scottish Cup tie. Bobby Stevenson is the only player to have achieved that feat since. (v Berwick Rangers on 4 February 1956). In season 1932/33 McGillivray was with Celtic and he joined Manchester United for 1933/34. In the modern age such credentials look impressive but Manchester United were far from being a glamorous club at this time.

As for poor Clackmannan, it can be truthfully written that there were worse teams in Scotland on that afternoon.

Ayr United: Hepburn, Willis, Fleming, Yorke, McLeod, McCall, Morgan, Tolland, McGillivray, Brae and Ferguson.

Clackmannan: Shepherd, Jenkins, Ferguson, Robertson, Hunter, Young, Forsyth, Reid, Gordon, Wright and Conacher.

AYR UNITED v. KILMARNOCK

29 April 1931   Scottish League First Division
Somerset Park

Ayr United entered the concluding League match of the 1930/31 season requiring at least one point to escape relegation. East Fife were already doomed to the Second Division whilst Hibs had finished their League campaign with twenty-five points. Ayr United had the same number of points as Hibs but had an inferior goal average. The difference was just 0.0397 of a goal. A 9-0 defeat away to Hearts on 28 February had now come back to haunt the club. In simple terms, it could be said that the aim was to glean a single point from the only remaining match. Yet there was a snag and it was potentially a large one. The last match was against Kilmarnock!

In the build-up to this Wednesday evening fixture, there were stories circulating that Kilmarnock would let Ayr United win. Such stories were ludicrous in the extreme. The rivalry was as intense then as it is in the modern age. It was wrongly reported that Hibs had not been in the Second Division before. They had, although not as a result of relegation. Before the game, a letter from the supporters' club was read to the players by Bob Hepburn. The letter was then pinned to the wall, not that any outside motivation was required.

It was a warm, sunny evening and the fans were entertained by the Maybole Burgh Band. This was all very pleasant, but the main business had yet to be conducted. Once underway, it could soon be seen that no home player was prepared to spare himself. In an early attack, Pearson Ferguson tested Killie goalkeeper Clemie with a low drive. Another foray around the Killie goal saw Wilf Armory try to chest the ball over the line, but he was beaten by weight of numbers. So much for the rumours about Kilmarnock lying down!

At the heart of the Ayr defence, Jimmy McLeod played the match with a bandage round his head. It was symbolic of the necessary determination. These reserves were called upon when Kilmarnock began to press. Hepburn had difficulty in containing a dangerous lob from Connell, and then Muir dribbled worryingly close to the Ayr goal. Distinct relief was felt when that bit of danger was cleared. It was not long before the home crowd were prematurely acclaiming a goal. Danny Tolland unleashed a drive at close range but the fans had not anticipated Clemie punching the ball over the crossbar in what was a magnificent save. The resultant corner-kick was then wasted when Tolland put it straight out. Andy McCall also tested the on-form Clemie, but a subsequent shot was so badly off-target that the 'keeper was not tested.

Bobby Yorke had to go off for treatment and he made an instant impact on his return when an effort went only just wide. Yet Kilmarnock were ever-willing to make a game of it and Hepburn had to look smart to save from Connell. The bandaged-head figure of Jimmy McLeod surged forward and hit a drive which took a deflection. It was a deflection that would have beaten lesser mortals but Clemie saved in typically brilliant fashion.

Three quick corners came the way of Ayr United. It was observed that Killie's superior tackling was instrumental in this development. It was further observed that there was no cohesion to Ayr's forward play.

In the second half, the home team had the handicap of facing the sun. Undeterred, an attacking policy was adopted right away and it almost paid the dividend of a goal. From close range, Alex Merrie struck the crossbar with a header. A subsequent attack looked promising until Pearson Ferguson delayed putting in a cross and the ball was forced out for a corner-kick. Unlike a first-half corner, Tolland crossed it perfectly and it is on record that 'Clemie

Ayr United 1   Kilmarnock 0
Tolland

Andy McCall.

defied numerous attempts to beat him' at this point. However, these close scrapes raised the excitement of the crowd. A different kind of excitement enveloped the crowd when the unmarked Connell fired the ball over the Ayr crossbar from close range. When play swung back, Alex Merrie headed over the Kilmarnock crossbar.

The Ayr supporters would have been delighted if the final whistle had blown at this stage. The vital point seemed to be in jeopardy when Jimmy McLeod looked to have conceded a penalty. However, no penalty was given, although the nerves were no doubt shredded just a little bit more. Strong Ayr attacking saw Kilmarnock yield a corner which was taken by Ferguson. The ball came over to Danny Tolland, who scored with a header which caused the crowd to 'yell themselves hoarse'. Fourteen minutes remained. In that time, survival hinged on avoiding the loss of two goals. With three minutes left, a Connell drive was pushed skyward by Hepburn. The ball then landed on top of the crossbar and hung there. Mercifully, it fell behind the goal. On the call of time, the stand patrons gave the team a deserved standing ovation.

It is an interesting thought that, at this time, Hibs were not even the best team in Leith. In beating Kilmarnock, Ayr United were instrumental in relegating Hibs and the final table showed Leith Athletic to be one of the clubs which narrowly survived.

First Division, Bottom Placings, 1930/31.

	P	W	D	L	F	A	Points
Leith Athletic	38	8	11	19	51	85	27
Ayr United	38	8	11	19	53	92	27
Hibs	38	9	7	22	49	81	25
East Fife	38	8	4	26	45	113	20

Ayr United: Hepburn, Robertson, Fleming, Yorke, McLeod, McCall, Tolland, Armory, Merrie, Brae and Ferguson.
Kilmarnock: Clemie, Leslie, Nibloe, Morton, Smith, McEwen, Connell, Muir, Maxwell, Napier and Aitken.

THIRD LANARK v. AYR UNITED

22 August 1933
Cathkin Park

Scottish League First Division

Prior to this game, the club-record individual scoring feat in a competitive fixture stood at five goals. The holder of that record was Jimmy Smith, who had achieved the feat no fewer than three times. On a Tuesday evening in the summer of 1933, Terry McGibbons created a new record, which still stands to this day, although Malky Morrison equalled it on 5 January 1946.

McGibbons was recruited from Irvine Meadow during the close season of 1933, only to receive the proverbial baptism of fire in senior football. The season opened with an 8-0 defeat at Aberdeen. This remains a club-record losing margin in an opening League game. A club director claimed that the memory of Armstrong scoring five for Aberdeen would soon be wiped out. He was right. Three days later, a 9-1 defeat was suffered against Rangers at Ibrox Park and Smith scored six! It was a totally appalling start to the season. Then Hearts were beaten 4-3 at Somerset Park in a match that saw McGibbons score twice. The scene was now set for the trip to face Third Lanark.

A heavy downpour marked the kick-off, although the weather conditions were not the prime concern. Third Lanark pressed straight into attack and took the lead through a McKenzie drive inside the first minute. In a counter-attack, Fally Rodger shot into the side net, then Terry McGibbons showed his intent with a hard shot which the goalkeeper managed to hold. Yet the next menacing attack was at the other end. Clarke, from fifteen yards, made it 2-0. Only six minutes had been played. Ayr goalkeeper George Wilson had to make good saves from Clarke and Lynas to prevent further arrears.

After eighteen minutes, Billy Brae released Fally Rodger, who crossed for Terry McGibbons to score. Lynas should then have re-established his side's two-goal lead but he somehow contrived to shoot over when well placed. This let-off signalled keen Ayr United pressure and Jimmy Brannan passed to McGibbons who made it 2-2, just three minutes after his first goal. Serious pressure was then mounted on the Third Lanark goal. Goalkeeper Taylor saved at point-blank range from McGibbons, Brae and Robertson. It was inspirational goalkeeping, although he was made to pay for his courage. In the last of those saves, he strained the sinews of his wrist and had to be replaced by right-back Simpson. It was a matter of misfortune to Third Lanark that the full-back had to complete the game in goal.

Ayr United were in no mood to show any sympathy. Johnny Holland made territory and played a one-two with Rodger before passing to McGibbons, who completed his hat trick with twenty-eight minutes on the clock.

At the start of the match, Ayr United had conceded a goal in the first minute and, on the resumption, it happened again. Right at the start of the second half, Breslin squared it at 3-3. The same player came close to covering himself in further glory when he was thwarted by a fine save from Wilson. In light of Third Lanark's plight, these were disturbing developments, yet when the chance was taken to next apply pressure on the rookie goalkeeper, Billy Brae looked on at the sight of his great shot being punched round the post. Jimmy Brannan was also beaten by a fine save. Simpson seemed to be unaware that he was supposed to be a right-back. A forward surge by McGibbons ended in the deputy 'keeper holding a shot on the line.

The involuntary goalkeeper had done extremely well to concede just one goal and was in defiant mood. However, the picture was about to change drastically with four Ayr United goals in the space of ten minutes. In the seventy-fifth minute, Andy McCall released Tommy

---

Third Lanark 3
McKenzie, Clarke, Breslin

Ayr United 7
McGibbons (6), McCall

Ayr United FC, 1933/34. From left to right, back row: Jimmy Dalziel (trainer), McCall, Currie, Fleming, Wilson, Ure, Holland. Front row: Robertson, Brae, McGibbons, Brannan, Rodger.

Robertson, who crossed for Terry McGibbons to score. Three minutes later, McGibbons netted a header and, again, the cross was supplied by Robertson. Four minutes then elapsed before Andy McCall made it 6-3 with a speculative shot. This was shortly after McKenzie had struck the Ayr crossbar. Three minutes after McCall's goal, McGibbons ran through to complete his double hat-trick.

The performance of McGibbons was neatly summed up in the following terms. 'Terry took his chances like the real opportunist he is. There is no wild driving over the bar with him. He shoots quickly, yet with a cool unerring skill, and even his worst shots are not far off the mark.'

When Third Lanark visited Somerset Park for the return League engagement, he scored four in a 5-1 win, making his final tally against the club an impressive ten goals.

Third Lanark: Taylor, Simpson, Warden, Blair, Robb, McLellan, Lynas, B. Clarke, McCulloch, McKenzie and Breslin.

Ayr United: Wilson, Falconer, Ure, McCall, Currie, Holland, Robertson, Brae, McGibbons, Brannan and Rodger.

CELTIC v. AYR UNITED

24 March 1934   Scottish League First Division
Celtic Park

Ayr United won both of the League games played against Celtic in season 1933/34, but the Celts did manage to win 3-2 in a second round Scottish Cup tie at Somerset Park. It is curious that one of the clubs in the second round draw was Galston, which was an Ayr United nursery club. Rather than having a reserve team, there was a farming-out arrangement with Galston. If the names had come out of the draw in a different order, there could have been a situation in which Ayr United faced what was tantamount to their reserve team. This is a convenient link to the fact that reserve outside-right Mair was called up from Galston to face Celtic at Celtic Park.

It will be recalled from an earlier page that, on the occasion of the convincing Ayr win at this venue in November 1922, the crowd figure was low. The situation here in 1934 was the same, and for the same reason. A journalist covering the game told his readers what they already knew. 'Parkhead crowds are small nowadays unless on a big occasion. There were only 6,000 present on Saturday.'

The home side attacked from the kick-off. They clearly dominated the opening minutes, yet failed to capitalise on that superiority. The game was one-sided at this early stage, although not quite entirely. There were a couple of raids into home territory. A clever flick from Terry McGibbons could not outwit Kennaway in the Celtic goal. Kennaway dropped the ball in a further raid, and he had cause to be grateful to McStay for getting the ball clear. (This was Jimmy McStay, not Willie McStay, whom Celtic had loaned to Ayr United in the past.)

The record books correctly imply that Jimmy McGrory was a most dangerous predator. It was therefore fortunate when Celtic winger Crum made a mess of a pass which was intended for the striker. Buchan then shot past from a good position and the Ayr goal was further threatened when McGrory made an attempt which was countered by a fine save from Bob Hepburn. A goal soon did come – at the other end! Johnny Holland was the quickest to react to a corner-kick. He met the ball first time and drove it past Kennaway.

Seventeen minutes had been played by the time Ayr scored. Naturally, this development stung Celtic back into attack. Hepburn dropped a cross, and the ensuing scramble involved the ball being headed off the goal line twice. Then Hepburn did magnificently to deflect Buchan's point-blank shot over the crossbar. These nervous moments became even more tense when, with Hepburn out of his goal, McGrory shot against the woodwork. Occasional counter-attacks relieved the pressure, yet there was more purpose to these attacks than merely keeping the heat off a beleaguered defence. So much so, that McGibbons scored with a low shot after neatly connecting with a pass.

The 2-0 half-time lead was more than satisfactory. Celtic's response, though, could almost have been scripted. The number of second-half corner-kicks conceded by Ayr United was described as 'remarkable'. With Celtic attacking, Ayr United managed to break again. In a right-wing move, Brae picked up possession from Mair before launching a high cross, which Kennaway dropped. The goalkeeper was immediately punished for this blunder as Terry McGibbons had the ball in the back of the net. Thirty-five minutes remained but, at 3-0 to Ayr United, the points were safe, lest Celtic should become sharper in front of goal. That the home team lacked fluency in attack was partly attributable to Davy Currie having what was described as 'a stranglehold' over McGrory. Celtic continued to set up the majority of the attacking moves, only to see them repelled.

Celtic 0   **Ayr United 3**
                                            Holland,
                                            McGibbons (2)

League Goals 1933/34	
McGibbons	35
Brae	11
Rodger	10
Robertson	7
Brannan	5
Holland	4
Ure	4
Taylor	3
Fisher	2
McCall	2
Currie	1
Mair	1
Dickson (Queen's Park)	1 own goal
T.G. Smith (Queen's Park)	1 own goal
Total	**87**

Terry McGibbons.

The proceedings had repercussions for Scotland's Wembley prospects. That match was three weeks away and it was a matter of concern that contenders such as Kennaway, McGonagle and McGrory had not made a good impression. However, Terry McGibbons had made a favourable impression and he was picked to go to Wembley as a travelling reserve. This was a tremendous honour in his first senior season, even though he was a spectator while Hughie Gallacher filled the striker's position in the course of a 3-0 defeat.

Celtic: Kennaway, Hogg, McGonagle, Geatons, McStay, Hughes, Crum, Buchan, McGrory, F. O'Donnell and H. O'Donnell.
Ayr United: Hepburn, Fleming, Ure, Taylor, Currie, Holland, Mair, Brae, McGibbons, Brannan and Rodger.

Ayr United v. King's Park

27 March 1937
Somerset Park

Scottish League Second Division

King's who? A brief explanation is appropriate. This was a Stirling-based club who played at a ground called Forthbank, although it was not on the site of Stirling Albion's ground in the present day; even though the identical name could give a contrary impression. In 1941, a stray Luftwaffe bomb landed on the original Forthbank ground and, on peace being restored, Stirling Albion emerged as a new club playing at a new ground, Annfield Park, by which time King's Park had been consigned to the pages of history.

The visit of King's Park comprised Ayr United's last home League match of the 1936/37 season and the winning result guaranteed promotion. Two away games then had to be played, the first of which brought the point required for the Second Division championship. It is to be hoped that there was an Ayr United statistician at this time. If so, the circumstances would have been a dream.

At the season's conclusion, 122 League goals had been scored. This remains a club record. The campaign also included a dozen consecutive League wins. This too remains a club record. Of the seventeen League games played at home, just a single point was dropped. It was almost perfection. Three of those home games involved Ayr United scoring eight goals.

The King's Park game was even easier than the scoreline suggested. Within several minutes, the competitive edge was gone. David Gemmell crossed from the by-line and Hyam Dimmer was able to get a foot to the ball to open the scoring after just two minutes. Dimmer then sent a high ball goalward and watched as it struck the inside of the crossbar before becoming lodged in the net – two goals in four minutes! This prompted Dimmer to chase a hat-trick. He was a footballing maestro, who loved to entertain the crowd with his substantial repertoire of skills. During his Ayr United career, he regularly gave the distinct impression that he preferred to make goalscoring easier for others. Against King's Park, though, he showed directness rather than the flamboyance which came naturally to him. At least this was true during the early part of the game. Inevitably, he reverted to his comedy routine. He brought out a good save in goalkeeper Wilson and, in a subsequent attack, he forced his way through a bunch of defenders, only to be dispossessed by Wilson after overhitting the ball. In pursuit of the elusive hat-trick, Dimmer later headed just over from a John Torbet cross. Minutes afterwards, an Albert Smith cross ended with the ball running along the crossbar and falling back into play, but McGibbons failed to capitalise. Before half-time, Dimmer was yet again thwarted by the goalkeeper's reflexes. The interval was reached with no further scoring.

Ayr United's attacking momentum rolled over into the second half. McGibbons, Gemmell and Torbet all had scoring chances, yet still the lead could not be increased. McGibbons squandered a further chance, although a marksman of his quality was not going to be denied indefinitely. From a throw-in on the right, Albert Smith headed the ball on to David Gemmell who, in turn, sent it on to Terry McGibbons, who scored easily. The club record for League goals in a season had previously stood at 117, scored in 1927/28. This sixty-eighth minute strike against King's Park put Ayr United's total at 117 League goals in 1936/37. Two minutes later came the goal which broke the record. A move involving Dimmer and Gemmell was finished by McGibbons. A less impressive statistic was that this goal was also the 100th League goal conceded by King's Park that season. The time lapse to the next goal was again two minutes. A Smith cross was diverted by McGibbons to Gemmell, who made it 5-0 with a header. Three goals in four minutes was an impressive statistic, but it really could have

---

Ayr United 5
Dimmer (2), McGibbons (2)
Gemmell

King's Park 0

League Goals 1936/37	
McGibbons	39
Dimmer	25
Torbet	22
Gemmell	16
Smith	11
Taylor	3
Fisher	2
Gibson	1
Strain	1
Richardson (Leith)	1 own goal
Maley (Morton)	1 own goal
Total	122

Hyam Dimmer.

been four goals in five minutes. Just a minute after the scoring burst, McGibbons shot over the crossbar with only the goalkeeper to beat. An act of mercy? Albert Smith put in a shot which the goalkeeper pushed against the crossbar, and the same player had the misfortune to see a further effort hit the same crossbar in the closing minutes. Hyam Dimmer had not yet given up his pursuit of a hat-trick, his last chance being a shot which the goalkeeper touched out for a fruitless corner. This match truly epitomised Ayr United's season.

Ayr United: R. Smith, Summers, Strain, Taylor, Currie, Mayes, A. Smith, Dimmer, McGibbons, Gemmell and Torbet.
King's Park: Wilson, Kennedy, Hogg, J. McDowell, W. Clark, McDonnell, Andrew, I. McDowell, Cassidy, Miller and Speedie.

AYR UNITED v. DUNDEE

30 April 1938   Scottish League First Division
Somerset Park

How could a 0-0 draw appear in a book of 'classic' matches? Admittedly, the match probably did stretch the definition of the word 'classic', but it was certainly a classic occasion. Yet it did not become a classic occasion until half-time. The confusion is easily explained.

Entering the final League Saturday, Morton were already guaranteed relegation. The question of who would join them in the drop looked to be a relatively straightforward issue as well. Queen of the South had to beat Rangers at Ibrox to stay up – even a draw was not enough. At Somerset Park, there was no sign of impending crisis until a strange development took place at half-time. An alphabetical key was printed in the programme in order that people could match it up with the half-time scoreboard. Letter 'A' signified the Rangers v. Queen of the South score, so that one went up first. Loud laughter then went up when the score was inserted as 0-3. There was a unanimous assumption that the score had been put in the wrong way round. Horrifyingly, the score was correct. The repercussions of a Queen of the South win meant that Ayr United required no less than a draw to escape relegation, whereas Dundee needed to win. The history of Ayr United is peppered with last game relegation scrapes, but only in 1938 and in 1998 have the club been in that situation while playing the other club in peril. In the now reasonable expectation of a Queen of the South win (they won 3-2), the Ayr United v. Dundee game was now fraught with danger.

Let's now turn back to the beginning of the match. At the outset, Ayr United had the disadvantage of playing against the sun and the wind, yet the elements did not deter an attacking emphasis. Lynch, in the visiting goal, had to look alert in getting to a Lewis Thow cross before Jimmy Yardley. Just afterwards, he had to look equally alert to save a header from Thow. At the other end, the Ayr goal was put under pressure from an unlikely source. Davy Currie attempted a headed clearance but misconnected with the result that it was a backward header. James Hall, better known as 'Henry', managed to make the save which avoided an embarrassing own goal.

Lewis Thow, who had reached the age of eighteen earlier in the month, continued to impose himself. He put in a cross which Lynch had to punch clear. Then Lynch distinguished himself by tipping over a full-blooded drive from Hyam Dimmer. Yet again, Thow was prominent. He hit the crossbar. A subsequent attack again nearly brought him a goal. He beat the goalkeeper in a race for possession, touched it past him, then watched as the ball went across the face of the goal. It was increasingly becoming apparent that it was going to be one of those days when the ball just would not go in. This argument is borne out by the fact that Terry McGibbons struck the post and David Gemmell put the rebound over. Just before half-time, McGibbons released Jimmy Yardley, who elected to pass to Thow, but the youngster's effort was off-target.

This was the proverbial game of two halves. The half-time score from Ibrox transformed a relatively meaningless game into a struggle for survival. In the opening minutes of the second half, further pressure was exerted on the Dundee goal. That was before the stark realisation of their situation stung the visiting players into a rally. However, it was was a rally that did not last. Lynch's goal was revisited and he saved from McGibbons. That save paled into insignificance when he brilliantly fisted over a Jock Mayes free-kick. Lynch continued his brilliant form in the face of intense attacking, although weak finishing also assisted him in the matter of keeping a clean goal. Dundee, even in their desperation, failed to gain any potency

Ayr United 0   Dundee 0

League Goals 1937/38	
McGibbons	20
Yardley	10
Dimmer	8
Smith	7
Steele	5
Devine	4
Gemmell	4
Thow	3
Taylor	2
Currie	1
Dyer	1
Mayes	1
Total	**66**

James 'Henry' Hall.

in attack and Hall, in the Ayr goal, was redundant for long spells.

In the opening weeks of 1937/38, Dundee had set the pace in the First Division, only to conclude the campaign as a relegated club. No club had ever been relegated from the Scottish First Division with a points total as high as thirty-two. The next time a club was relegated from Scottish football's top sphere with as high a total was in 1975/76. Again, the total was thirty-two; again, the club was Dundee; and again, Ayr United were involved, even though it was indirectly. Remember that it was two points for a win in the seasons mentioned here. The completed First Division table for 1937/38 showed that many clubs had sailed closely to the relegation wind. It is interesting to reflect that, on the basis of three points for a win, Ayr United would have gone down.

First Division, Bottom Placings, 1937/38.

	P	W	D	L	F	A	Points
Queen's Park	38	11	12	15	59	74	34
Hamilton Accies	38	13	7	18	81	76	33
St Mirren	38	14	5	19	58	66	33
Clyde	38	10	13	15	68	78	33
Queen of the South	38	11	11	16	58	71	33
Ayr United	38	9	15	24	66	85	33
Kilmarnock	38	12	9	17	65	91	33
Dundee	38	13	6	19	70	74	32
Morton	38	6	3	29	64	127	15

Ayr United: Hall, Dyer, Strain, Taylor, Currie, Mayes, McGibbons, Dimmer, Yardley, Gemmell and Thow.
Dundee: Lynch, Rennie, Richards, Cowie, Morgan, Smith, Boyd, McMenemy, Coats, Baxter and Roberts.

AYR UNITED v. HAMILTON ACCIES

2 September 1939   Scottish League First Division
Somerset Park

'SHOCK AYR RAIDS ON ACCIES'
'CLARK GETS IN THREE DIRECT HITS'

The fighting connotations in the headlines above were appropriate. Both appeared in a newspaper dated Sunday 3 September 1939, the day on which war was declared. On the Saturday, the evacuation of children from heavily populated areas was being undertaken. Military demands and general duties also prevailed on a populace to whom football was not a major priority on 2 September. Yet, despite the surreal air to it all, football took place as scheduled on that day.

So far that season, the First Division had yielded Ayr United one win and three defeats. In light of the international situation, the visit of Hamilton Accies was to constitute the club's last First Division fixture of the season.

In November 1987, a letter was sent to Ayr United by Jimmy Marshall, the scorer of two goals in the match featured here. In the letter, he attempted to name the team which had faced Hamilton. This was close to a half-century later and it is commendable that he only got one name wrong. He named Dyer at right-back, but that position had been filled by Craik. The letter continued: 'The referee was Peter Craigmyle, the manager was Frank Thompson and the trainer was Eddie Summers'. These details were all accurate and the by now elderly Marshall modestly made no mention of his goals in the game.

The exchanges were even for the first twenty-five minutes, despite the fact that the Accies played the more polished football. However, such is the nature of the game that Ayr United then found the back of the net. A glancing pass from Jacky Clark (nicknamed Elkie) was met first time by Jimmy Marshall, who dispatched it into the net in glorious style. Five minutes later, Clark scored a goal which was considered to be even better. He got possession out of a scrum of players before hitting a strike which 'beat Campbell hollow'.

Eight minutes into the second half, a through ball from John McKenzie caught out the Hamilton defence and Jacky Clark was able to put it past the outrushing goalkeeper. It took Clark two more minutes to complete his hat-trick. He did so with a header from a McGibbons corner-kick. Four goals up with only ten minutes of the second half played! The Accies, as anticipated, did not recover. In fact, their situation deteriorated. Peter Smith hit a drive with such force that Campbell dropped it, and Marshall took the opportunity to score. Not long afterwards, Peter Smith made it 6-0, following a corner-kick. Twenty minutes remained when Darge scored for the visitors in a breakaway. Thereafter, the closing stages were dull due to a slackening off.

Had Ayr United continued to emphasise their superiority with more goals, it would not have made any difference. The declaration of war brought the League grinding to a halt. Players' contracts were immediately cancelled by the Scottish Football Association and, since the Ayr United players were full-time, this rendered them unemployed. Not that they were unemployed for long – work and military demands made sure of that. Jacky Clark had signed his soon-to-be-void contract on 4 May 1939, and it was supposed to run until 30 April 1940. As a consequence, he found himself playing for the club on less princely terms than those agreed. These terms should have rewarded him with £4 per week during the playing season, together with a further £1 for appearing in the first team and a bonus of £1 per point.

Ayr United 6   Hamilton Accies 1
Marshall (2), Clark (3), Smith   *Darge*

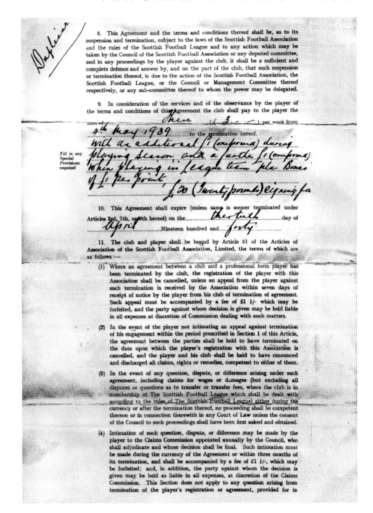

8. This Agreement and the terms and conditions thereof shall be, as to its suspension and termination, subject to the laws of the Scottish Football Association and the rules of the Scottish Football League and to any action which may be taken by the Council of the Scottish Football Association or any deputed committee, and in any proceedings by the player against the club, it shall be a sufficient and complete defence and answer by, and on the part of the club, that such suspension or termination thereof, is due to the action of the Scottish Football Association, the Scottish Football League, or the Council or Management Committee thereof respectively, or any sub-committee thereof to whom the power may be delegated.

9. In consideration of the services and of the observance by the player of the terms and conditions of this Agreement the club shall pay to the player the sum of ~~~~ *There* (£3 -) per week from *4th May 1939* to the termination hereof. *with an additional £1 (one pound) during playing season and a further £1 (one pound) when playing in league team plu Bonus of £1 per point. £20 (Twenty pounds) signing fee*

10. This Agreement shall expire (unless same is sooner terminated under Articles 3rd, 7th, or 8th hereof) on the *thirtieth* day of *April* Nineteen hundred and *forty*.

11. The club and player shall be bound by Article 51 of the Articles of Association of the Scottish Football Association, Limited, the terms of which are as follows :—

(1) Where an agreement between a club and a professional form player has been terminated by the club, the registration of the player with this Association shall be cancelled, unless an appeal from the player against such termination is received by the Association within seven days of receipt of notice by the player from his club of termination of agreement. Such appeal must be accompanied by a fee of £1 1/- which may be forfeited, and the party against whom decision is given may be held liable in all expenses at discretion of Commission dealing with such matters.

(2) In the event of the player not intimating an appeal against termination of his engagement within the period prescribed in Section 1 of this Article, the agreement between the parties shall be held to have terminated on the date upon which the player's registration with this Association is cancelled, and the player and his club shall be held to have renounced and discharged all claims, rights or remedies, competent to either of them.

(3) In the event of any question, dispute, or difference arising under such agreement, including claims for wages or damages (but excluding all disputes or questions as to transfer or transfer fees, where the club is in membership of The Scottish Football League which shall be dealt with according to the rules of The Scottish Football League) either during the currency or after the termination thereof, no proceeding shall be competent thereon or in connection therewith in any Court of Law unless the consent of the Council to such proceedings shall have been first asked and obtained.

(4) Intimation of such question, dispute, or difference may be made by the player to the Claims Commission appointed annually by the Council, who shall adjudicate and whose decision shall be final. Such intimation must be made during the currency of the Agreement or within three months of its termination, and shall be accompanied by a fee of £1 1/-, which may be forfeited; and, in addition, the party against whom the decision is given may be held as liable in all expenses, at discretion of the Claims Commission. This Section does not apply to any question arising from termination of the player's registration or agreement, provided for in

An extract from Jacky Clark's 1939/40 contract.

Football did continue in Scotland. The leagues were restructured on a regional basis. At the conclusion of the 1939/40 season, the Ayr United board decided to close the club down for the duration. In the summer of 1940, Jacky Clark was fixed up by Hamilton Accies. In addition to his hat-trick against them on the eve of war, he also scored home and away against them in the Regional League. However, he moved to Third Lanark within two months of going to Hamilton. Thereafter, the player was lost to Ayr United, and it is difficult not to reflect on the career he could have had at the club, had it not been for the intervention of war. He scored twenty-six goals in the Regional League in 1939/40, despite the observation in March that he had lost the capacity for scoring goals due to working long shifts which ended at six o'clock on a Saturday morning. Nevertheless, he had paid a handsome return for his £20 signing-on fee.

Ayr United: Hall, Craik, Strain, Cox, Whiteford, Mayes, McGibbons, McKenzie, Clark, Smith and Marshall.

Hamilton Accies: Campbell, Wallace, Scott, McKenzie, Low, Jarvie, Hay, Kennedy, Darge, Harrison and Devine.

AYR UNITED v. STENHOUSEMUIR

5 January 1946   Scottish League 'B' Division
Somerset Park

This remains a club record League win and Malky Morrison's six goals equalled the club record for an individual in a competitive match. (See earlier entry: Third Lanark v. Ayr United on 22 August 1933.) Morrison was a sharp striker, whose name is in the list of the club's top ten scorers of all time, but, in this match, his cause was helped by a young trialist goalkeeper who suffered badly from an increasing loss of confidence. At least his trialist status protected his identity. He played under the guise of 'Newman'. Ayr United, too, had a trialist in this match; an outside-left, who was also listed as 'Newman'.

At this time, Malky Morrison was a sergeant in the Highland Light Infantry and he was due to be demobbed later that month. He was conveniently stationed at Maryhill Barracks, therefore Ayr United were not deprived of his services. This may have been convenient for Ayr United, but the Stenhousemuir defenders would have had a less torrid afternoon if Malky had been stationed overseas.

Just four minutes had been played when Morrison got possession from John Malcolm, and then ran on to put the ball past the advancing goalkeeper. After four more minutes had elapsed, Tommy McGuigan made ground before passing to George Gillan, who promptly dispatched the ball past the young trialist. A forceful drive from Morrison then came back off the underside of the crossbar. It is interesting to reflect that, but for a matter of inches, he would have scored seven. Yet the third Ayr United goal was inevitable. George Gillan was pulled down by a cynical tackle for a penalty kick, which Peter Smith converted. This goal was timed at twenty-two minutes.

Further misfortune befell Stenhousemuir, quite apart from the loss of goals. Centre-half Syme injured himself while tackling. He left the field and did not return, thereby leaving his team short-handed. The visiting defence was beleaguered enough without the loss of a player in a key role. Now, the consequences were predictable.

Visibly showing nerves, the goalkeeper dropped the ball. It fell to Morrison, who was standing on the by-line, yet still managed to score from an angle which looked tight to the point of impossible. Shortly before half-time, he completed the first of his hat-tricks to make it 5-0. He evaded a despairing tackle before running on to fire the ball home.

The second half though, was to prove even more one-sided than the first. An old Ayr United trait soon surfaced; the trait whereby the team's superiority is manifested by showing off whenever there is a substantial lead. Despite this, the hunger for goals was not totally lost. With fifty-seven minutes played, a well-placed corner-kick gave Morrison the chance to make it 6-0. The chance was gratefully accepted. In a rare attack, Stenhousemuir managed to score with a shot from Beveridge, which initially looked as if it was going to drop over the crossbar. It did not take long to restore the six-goal advantage. Morrison made it 7-1 just a minute later. The vast superiority was further emphasised when a handling offence resulted in Ayr United's second penalty of the match. Once more, Peter Smith did the needful. Morrison proceeded to make it 9-1, and the final ignominy for the visitors came in the final minute, when Tommy McGuigan made it a resounding 10-1 annihilation.

The earlier League engagement between the clubs had taken place at Stenhousemuir's Ochilview Park on 13 October 1945. It was the occasion of a 6-0 Ayr United win, in which Malky Morrison scored four goals. Ten goals by an individual against the one club over the two League meetings that season! Elderly supporters will tell you that Malky Morrison used to react excitedly whenever he scored. He simply loved scoring.

Ayr United 10   **Stenhousemuir 1**
Morrison (6), Gillan, Smith (2)   *Beveridge*
McGuigan

Ayr United FC – 29 December 1945, one week before the double-figure rout. From left to right, back row: W. Hunter (assistant trainer), Kirkland, McGuigan, Brown, McNeil, Malcolm, Jimmy Dalziel (trainer). Front row: Henderson, Kelly, Morrison, Calder, Gillan, Harper.

League Goals 1945/46	
Morrison	29
Malcolm	10
Smith	7
Melvin	6
Gillan	4
Harper	3
McGuigan	3
Leitch	2
Henderson	2
Calder	1
Hunter	1
McNeil	1
Total	69

Ayr United: Brown, Kirkland, Kelly, Henderson, Smith, Calder, McGuigan, Malcolm, Morrison, Gillan and 'Newman'.

Stenhousemuir: 'Newman', Marshall, Geddes, Anderson, Syme, Beveridge, Arbuckle, Crighton, Whyte, Smith and Duncan.

Ayr United v. Motherwell

7 October 1950   Scottish League Cup Semi-Final
Ibrox Park

Although this match resulted in an Ayr United defeat, it was also the first occasion on which an Ayr United team reached the semi-final stage of a major cup competition. It was also close to being the first occasion of reaching a major final, since a 3-2 lead was held right up until the eighty-third minute.

A Saturday afternoon kick-off was conducive to a large crowd, and it is known that more than 45,000 people passed through the turnstiles. Unfortunately, their eyes then looked out on a playing surface which was described as 'bad'. However, one journalist described the pitch in more poetic terms: 'When referee Livingstone and one of his linesmen came out to inspect the nets, the pair of them picked their way from turf to turf as though they were crossing the stepping stones at Overmills'. This local reference would have been well understood by residents of Ayr's Holmston district, yet the message was still clear to everybody.

Prior to the tie, Ayr United received an abundance of good luck telegrams from such diverse sources as Kilmarnock FC, Inverness Caledonian FC, Coylton Juveniles and a Raith Rovers supporters' club, who addressed their greetings to former Raith players Ian Crawford and Hugh Goldie, both of whom stood to get their name on the scoresheet. Yet the main spur for victory probably emanated from the enthusiasm of the black-and-white bedecked thousands.

Playing with the advantage of the elements, Ayr United sensationally took a third-minute lead. Goalkeeper Hamilton emerged to intercept the in-rushing Ross Henderson, who succeeded in crossing the ball. The cross was missed by Ian Crawford, but Hugh Goldie was tidily placed to score with a low shot. Several minutes later, the enthusiasm of the Ayr supporters was stifled when Andy Nesbit was carried off with a knee injury. More than twenty minutes were to pass before he was able to rejoin the game.

Motherwell inside-forwards Jim Forrest and Jimmy Watson began to take an active role, and this caused the Ayr United defence some anxiety. In the fourteenth minute, Norrie McNeil conceded a corner-kick. As corner-kicks go, it was not struck sweetly. The ball did not rise above head height, and when Willie Fraser attempted a headed clearance, he failed to get enough distance on it. It was then met by the head of Jimmy Watson, who succeeded in equalising.

At this stage, the Ayr attack was depleted, as Goldie had dropped back to cover for the departed Nesbit. Alec Beattie and Willie Gallacher both attempted solo runs, only to find the road to goal blocked. It was as if they were both attempting the work of two men in order to compensate for their absent colleague. A stonewall penalty was then denied. Hamilton dropped a Fraser lob and he got involved with Ian Crawford in a chase for possession. With the ball running loose, Crawford found his mobility restricted by having the goalkeeper's arms wrapped tightly round his legs.

Johnny Aitkenhead gave Motherwell a 2-1 lead in the thirty-eighth minute. However, the Ayr United cause was aided by the reappearance of Andy Nesbit. Initially, Nesbit was a passenger on the wing but, at the start of the second half, he was back in his familiar position, with only a minor trace of a limp. The credit for this was surely down to the good work of club trainer Hugh Good. By now, a strong wind was being faced. Not that the elements deterred excursions into Motherwell territory. Alec Beattie beat full-back Willie Kilmarnock before delivering a cross in the direction of Ross Henderson. As with the incident leading up

---

Ayr United 3
Goldie, Crawford (2)

Motherwell 4
Watson (2), Aitkenhead (2)

League Cup Goals 1950/51	
Crawford	13
Gallacher	5
Henderson	2
McMenemy	2
Beattie	1
Goldie	1
Total	**24**

to the opening goal, Hamilton came rushing out. A further similarity was that Henderson again won possession before putting in a cross. This time, the ball came off the face of the crossbar to allow Ian Crawford to effortlessly touch it in to make it 2-2. One account stated that he 'walked the ball home'.

Right from the kick-off, Ayr United regained possession. Alec Beattie again beat Willie Kilmarnock before running on to unleash a ferocious shot, which went across the face of the goal. Archie Shaw desperately attempted a clearance, which struck team-mate Andy Paton and then shot skyward. Ian Crawford reacted quickly by jumping to head Ayr United 3-2 in front. What a start to the second half! Crawford's two goals came in the first three minutes after the interval.

As the game progressed, 'The Steelmen' became increasingly desperate in their efforts. Wave after wave of attack went in the direction of Len Round's goal and were repeatedly repelled. Full-backs John Duncan and Alec Perrie were magnificent, as was centre-half Norrie McNeil.

Len Round was experiencing difficulty in taking goal-kicks against the wind, therefore this task became the responsibility of Norrie McNeil. One such kick landed at the feet of Motherwell's Andy Paton, who ran past Ian Crawford before giving possession to Johnny Aitkenhead. McNeil slipped while attempting to tackle Aitkenhead and the latter took full advantage of the easy chance presented to him to make it 3-3. Having taken the goal-kick, Norrie McNeil had been caught out of position. The slip had been caused by having to sprint from the six-yard line to try to avert the impending danger. A bad surface was also a contributory factor. This happened just seven minutes before the end. It was a dreadfully disheartening development. Two minutes afterwards, the disappointment was compounded when Jimmy Watson 'glided in the winning goal' for Motherwell. It is on record that 'Watson was almost buried in the Ibrox mud by his back-slapping mates'.

Ayr United: Round, Duncan, Perrie, Fraser, McNeil, Nesbit, Henderson, Gallacher, Crawford, Goldie and Beattie.

Motherwell: Hamilton, Kilmarnock, Shaw, McLeod, Paton, Redpath, Hunter, Forrest, Kelly, Watson and Aitkenhead.

AYR UNITED v. MOTHERWELL

10 March 1951
Somerset Park

Scottish Cup Quarter-Finals
Attendance: 22,152

In 1951, Ayr United's Scottish Cup campaign began with a 2-1 away win over Stirling Albion in front of an attendance of 12,579. The draw for the second round then entailed a tie against Queen's Park at Hampden Park and it was observed that: 'The gate is not likely to be a good one because of counter attractions'. There was some substance to that comment when it is considered that Rangers and Hibs, the two strongest sides in Scotland at the time, were drawn together at nearby Ibrox Park. Whether the Celtic v. Duns tie was a counter attraction was questionable. Yet Ayr United beat Queen's Park 3-1 before a crowd recorded as 23,000. To this point, Jimmy Baker had scored all five of the club's Scottish Cup goals. The quarter-final draw then brought Motherwell to Somerset Park. It was an all-ticket tie in which the crowd figure was again impressive.

Earlier in the season, Ayr United had been close to glory against Motherwell in the League Cup. 'B' Division status had not daunted the Ayr players in face of their supposedly more illustrious opponents. This time, with ground advantage, there was a genuine optimism that the club could at last find a way through to the last four of the Scottish Cup.

After the kick-off, there was no time to settle in. Rather than having tentative opening exchanges, the action exploded in the second minute. Ian Crawford and Willie Japp worked a move which culminated in Jimmy Baker being set up with a glorious chance. The chance was lost, due to Baker taking the time to try to manoeuvre the ball onto his preferred left foot. In the next minute, Crawford lobbed the ball in the direction of the Motherwell goal. Again, a chance fell Baker's way, but was wasted as he again tried to move so he could shoot from his left foot.

'The Steelmen' reacted to these misses by applying pressure on the Ayr goal. Len Round saved well from Jim Forrest and Johnny Aitkenhead. Then, on the quarter-hour mark, a goal was conceded. Norrie McNeil attempted a header back to Len Round, but Jimmy Watson intervened sufficiently to get a boot on the ball and divert it into the net. The lead was maintained for just two minutes. From a range of about twenty yards, Jimmy Baker got possession. This time he did succeed in setting it up for his left foot. He then rifled it past John Johnston in the Motherwell goal. It maintained his record of having scored all of Ayr United's Scottish Cup goals so far in 1951.

This goal invigorated Baker. He hit a low cross across the face of goal. It was missed by everyone, but these were still uncomfortable moments for the defenders in the claret-and-amber shirts. Ayr United again pressed forward. This time, Baker was halted by a leg-breaking tackle from Archie Shaw. Not until January 1952 did Baker next play first-team football for Ayr United, and he was freed at the end of the 1951/52 season. In the short term, it was necessary to complete this tie with ten men. Had there been any justice, Motherwell, too, would have played on with ten men. Controversially, the referee did not consider Shaw's appalling tackle to be worthy of a dismissal.

Norrie McNeil, in his role as captain, instructed Willie Japp to move from the right wing to fill the now vacant centre-forward position. Ian Crawford was then left with extra ground to cover on the right flank. Whether as a result of a tactical masterstroke, or not, Ian Crawford barged past three defenders and touched the ball into the net via the underside of the crossbar. This goal came ten minutes before half-time and there existed the possibility that Ayr United would be carried through this tie by a gut determination.

Ayr United 2
Baker, Crawford

Motherwell 2
Watson, Forrest

Norrie McNeil.

On the resumption, it was soon evident that the object was to do somewhat better than just hanging on. Willie Japp, in particular, waged havoc on the visiting defence. Sadly, the elusive tie-killing goal did not materialise. Frustratingly, with half an hour left, Johnny Aitkenhead crossed for Jim Forrest to make it 2-2 from close in.

Still Ayr United would not relent. It was noticed that Alec Beattie was revelling in the extra space allowed by a four-man forward line. With five minutes remaining, a low cross from Japp saw Ian Harper fail to connect for what would have been a certain winner. The ball continued on its course towards Beattie, who made a desperate, but unsuccessful, attempt to turn it into the net.

·What happened after this honourable draw? The answer is that Ayr United lost 2-1 in the midweek replay. Not until the final minute of extra time was the killer goal conceded.

Ayr United: Round, Leckie, Perrie, Cairns, McNeil, Nesbit, Japp, Crawford, Baker, Harper and Beattie.

Motherwell: Johnston, Kilmarnock, Shaw, McLeod, Paton, Redpath, Watters, Forrest, Kelly, Watson and Aitkenhead.

Ayr United v. Dumbarton

13 August 1952   Scottish League Cup Sectional Tie
Somerset Park

This remains a record score in the history of the League Cup competition, although it has since been equalled once. That was on 11 August 1993, when a tie at Fir Park, Motherwell, ended Albion Rovers 1 Partick Thistle 11. The rout of Dumbarton also saw a milestone goal. One of Jim Fraser's strikes comprised Ayr United's 100th League Cup goal. (It is almost certain that nobody was aware of that statistic at the time.)

The 1952/53 season began with Ayr United in the same League Cup section as Stirling Albion, Dumbarton and Dundee United. The opening game was at Stirling, where the tie kicked off in heavy rain on an already waterlogged pitch – in August! Stirling Albion won 2-0 and, had it not been for the brilliance of goalkeeper Len Round, the scale of defeat would have been of less sensible proportions.

Prior to the midweek visit of Dumbarton, there was a lot of grumbling around Somerset Park. This was in response to the Ayr team being read out over the loudspeakers. The selection was unchanged from Stirling. It is a clear understatement to suggest that manager Archie Anderson had his judgement questioned. Football is a fickle game. Just how fickle was about to emerge.

The first goal came with five minutes played. Jacky Robertson hit a perfect pass to Willie Japp, who struck a cross-cum-shot which ended up in the net. Ten minutes later, Japp was involved in the next goal. His long pass deceived centre-half Whyte, thereby leaving Jim Fraser with an easy task in scoring. In the next minute, it was 3-0. Andy Nesbit fed the ball to Mike McKenna, who crossed it for Jim Fraser to score with a first-time strike.

Jim Fraser proved that he was adept at providing goals as well. In an incisive run, he beat two defenders and then crossed for Willie Japp to fire past Paton in the Dumbarton goal. Fraser, again in the thick of the action, had the misfortune to strike a post during a goalmouth scramble. Yet his misfortune was Jacky Robertson's good fortune, when the latter shot home the rebound to take the score to 5-0 with forty minutes played.

One of the match reports likened Ayr United to a goal machine. In the second half, the goal machine remained well oiled. Approximately one minute after the break, Jacky Robertson netted with a header from a Mike McKenna corner-kick. In keeping with the trend, the goals just kept on coming. Jim Fraser got his hat-trick by heading home the rebound after a Willie Japp shot had struck the crossbar. A typical burst of speed from Japp was then followed by an excellent cross, which Fraser headed past Paton for his own fourth goal and Ayr United's eighth. The goals continued to mount. Mike McKenna threw himself at an Andy Nesbit cross, and he connected to make it 9-0.

Given the circumstances, it was remarkable that Dumbarton even remotely remembered the route to goal. Yet Donegan, their right-winger, beat Len Round with a shot which found its way into the top corner of the net. The response to this was Jim Fraser setting up Japp to clinch his hat-trick. At 10-1, it may have been thought that there would be an easing up because double-figures had been reached. This was not the case. Joe Hutton was pulled down while advancing on the Dumbarton goal. As a consequence, a penalty-kick was given, which Hutton took himself to conclude the scoring at 11-1. This meant that all five home forwards had scored.

A fortnight later, the teams met in the return tie at Boghead Park. Somehow, Ayr United contrived to fare no better than a 1-1 draw, not that it mattered. Stirling Albion progressed to the quarter-finals by winning the section easily.

Ayr United 11   **Dumbarton 1**
Japp (3), J. Fraser (4), Robertson (2)   *Donegan*
McKenna, Hutton

Ayr United FC 1952/53. From left to right, back row: McKnight, Cairns, Round, Leckie, Strickland, Rodger. Front row: Japp, W.Fraser, J.Fraser, Robertson, McKenna. The blond-haired schoolboy in the centre of the the picture is Ian Ure, a local lad who went on to achieve fame with Arsenal and Manchester United.

League Cup Milestone Goals

Number 100 – Jim Fraser v. Dumbarton at Somerset Park, 13/8/52
Number 200 – Peter Price v. Montrose at Somerset Park, 13/8/58
Number 300 – Sam McMillan v. Third Lanark at Cathkin Park, 6/9/65
Number 400 – Rikki Fleming v. Dunfermline Athletic at East End Park, 9/8/75
Number 500 – Darren Henderson v. Rangers at Ibrox, 4/9/96

Ayr United: Round, W. Fraser, McKeown, Cairns, McNeil, Nesbit, Japp, Robertson, J. Fraser, Hutton and McKenna.
Dumbarton: Paton, McNee, Ferguson, Shaw, Whyte, Tait, Donegan, Malloch, Maxwell, Scott and Finnie.

AYR UNITED v. BRECHIN CITY

30 April 1956
Somerset Park

Scottish League 'B' Division

The scoreline to this game may not look especially earth-shattering, yet this Monday evening game drew an attendance of anything between 12,000 and 15,000 – depending on which newspaper people cared to believe.

To understand the importance of the occasion, it is necessary to hark back to the summer of 1945. With VE day having passed, it was decided that the Scottish League structure for 1945/46 would be the responsibility of seven men. They were three delegates from the Southern League, three delegates from the North-Eastern League and James Bowie, chairman of the Southern League. (Not to be confused with Douglas Bowie, the former Ayr United chairman, who was president of the Scottish Football Association from 1937 until 1945.) Getting the Scottish Leagues back into a national structure, rather than the wartime regional structure, was a praiseworthy notion. Unfortunately, the ensuing carve-up brought eternal shame on the seven men. Ayr United had been closed down in the summer of 1940 and, on the resumption, found themselves put into Division 'B' in 1945, rather than Division 'A'. The last completed peacetime table of 1938/39 saw the club finish above Third Lanark, St Mirren and Queen's Park, all of whom were granted a place in the new upper tier. Morton, who had finished in the bottom half of the Second Division in 1938/39, found themselves being mystically promoted in 1945. In effect, Ayr United were relegated by a combination of the war and the highly questionable judgement of a group of administrators. It took until 1956 for the injustice to be corrected.

Entering the final League match of 1955/56, one point was required to guarantee promotion along with champions Queen's Park. The large crowd turned out in the reasonable expectation that the visit of Brechin City made this an attainable aim. Perhaps, though, the anticipation was tempered by the knowledge that Ayr United had lost a League fixture at Brechin in the previous month.

Heavy was the responsibility to please the crowd. It is a fact that the importance of the occasion caused a number of fixtures to be postponed in the Ayr Domino League! As the game progressed, the fans managed to play a part by roaring encouragement at every attack on the Brechin goal. Gradually, the corner-kick count began to mount. One such kick eventually brought a reward. When the ball came over, it was headed away by Brechin defender Paterson, but he only cleared it to the unmarked John Traynor, who drove it through a packed goalmouth and into the net with twenty minutes played. The fans were ecstatic.

The visitors were not content to wilt. There was a pattern of attack being responded to by counter-attack. By half-time, the slender lead was still intact but, on returning to the field, a strong determination in the home team was soon evident. A strong drive from Bobby Stevenson typified the prevailing attitude, although he was denied by an exceptional save from Curran in the Brechin goal. John Traynor was then denied when he took a free-kick, which hit the face of the crossbar before being unceremoniously cleared. With fifty-three minutes played, a corner-kick was only partially cleared. This allowed Sam McMillan to gain possession and score with a low drive. At 2-0, promotion was within sight, and the fans knew it. Two minutes later, Peter Price got the ball in the net. It was just a pity that he had used his hands as the means of propulsion.

To the credit of the Brechin players, they fought their way back into the match. Former Ayr United player Norman Christie went frighteningly close with a low shot. At this stage, the

---

Ayr United 2
Traynor, McMillan

Brechin City 0

NEIL
McBAIN

EX - AYR UNITED PLAYER.
SCOTTISH INTERNATIONAL.

MANAGER.
AYR UNITED F.C.
1955 -1956.

Neil McBain, manager, 1955/56.

coolness of centre-half Mike Gallagher was mainly attributable to keeping the Ayr goal intact. On resuming the offensive, Alec Beattie was marginally too high with a strong drive then, in the next minute, he succeeded in beating the goalkeeper, only for the ball to strike left-back Hodge and deflect over the crossbar. By the closing minutes, the fast pace had at last subsided, yet Warrender did manage to find a burst of pace to get through and test Len Round with a low drive.

The final whistle was the signal for the fans to engulf the field. Only with difficulty did the Ayr players reach the home dressing room. A chant of 'We want Neilly' went up. Manager Neil McBain responded by appearing in the directors' box to acclaim the mass in front of him. Some of the directors celebrated in a novel way after finding a bowler hat which belonged to one of their number, Jimmy Frew. They had a game of football with it!

Word of Ayr United's promotion spread very quickly throughout the town, and some of the excesses of celebration took place far from the ground. At last, the injustice of the shameful post war carve-up had been avenged.

Ayr United: Round, Leckie, Thomson, Traynor, Gallagher, Haugh, Japp, McMillan, Price, Stevenson and Beattie.

Brechin City: Curran, Paterson, Hodge, Rennie, Aitken, Christie, Warrender, Muir, 'Junior', Gray and Duncan.

AYR UNITED v. RANGERS

12 January 1957   Scottish League First Division
Somerset Park

The 1956/57 season was not a kind one for Ayr United. It was a season of struggle, which brought relegation at the end of it. The January visit of Rangers, who were on course to retain the Championship, was an intimidating prospect. An early handicap in the match further compounded the trepidation. Yet this match contained an incident which was unforgettable. Those who were present can still clearly recall 'that goal'.

Injury worries caused manager Jacky Cox to delay his team selection, although a 5-2 defeat away to Raith Rovers on the previous Saturday may also have caused him to be studious about the best combination to stem what was expected to be a blue-and-white tide. When the line-up was made known, the mood of the supporters was not uplifted. In fact, the despair deepened further. Regular goalkeeper Len Round was replaced by the relatively inexperienced Willie Travers. It was generally wondered how he would fare against a Rangers team which was hungry for points in order to catch up with Hearts in the quest for the Championship.

George Young won the toss-up, and he booked the wind advantage for his Rangers team. As anticipated, the visitors soon pressed eagerly into attack. Johnny Hubbard tore at the Ayr United defence with a series of incisive runs. This was in keeping with the generally expected trend. Yet Travers dealt capably with the shots and crosses that came his way, and he seemed to grow in stature during the process. Then, in the thirteenth minute, Johnny Hubbard broke through and he was in the act of shooting when Bobby Thomson came in with a saving tackle. Thomson's ribs crashed into Hubbard's boot. The subsequent injury meant that Thomson took no further part in the game, leaving ten men to face Rangers for seventy-seven minutes. The job was difficult enough with eleven.

In the ensuing reshuffle, young John Telfer dropped back from left-half to take up the left-back position formerly occupied by Bobby Thomson. Jimmy Whittle reverted from inside-left to occupy the position formerly occupied by Telfer, and the consequence was a forward line which was reduced to four men.

The pressure on the Ayr defence continued. Willie Travers, Alex Paterson and Gordon Brice all shone in face of what was thrust at them. Let's not forget John Telfer either. He had been signed from Douglas Water Thistle the previous month, and had made his first-team debut just ten days before the visit of Rangers. His inexperience did not prevent him from matching Alex Scott, the international winger he was in direct opposition to. Overall, the defending was inspired, while the Ayr cause was further helped by the wayward shooting of the Rangers forwards. It all combined to make the first half scoreless.

Rangers had the wind advantage in the first half, therefore Ayr United would be likely to benefit from the elements in the second half. However, in a matter of minutes the wind dropped, and this rendered any advantage minimal. Fate seemed to be conspiring against the home team. This was all the more true when Peter Price suffered a head injury and had to leave the field for several minutes, during which time the home side battled on with nine men.

As the onslaught continued, George Young ventured upfield to add his weight to the visiting attack. It was to no avail. The Ayr defence repelled everything in a fashion which suggested that maybe, just maybe, it would be possible to hold out for a draw.

With barely ten minutes remaining, Ayr United were awarded a free-kick, for which Gordon Brice took the responsibility. Naturally, he took his time when placing the ball. At that point, someone in the Rangers team complained that the ball should have been further back.

Ayr United 1   Rangers 0
Japp

League Goals 1956/57	
Price	21
Beattie	4
McMillan	4
Paton	4
Whittle	4
Boden	3
Japp	3
Stevenson	2
Haugh	1
Murray	1
Thomson	1
Total	**48**

This was ideal. It gave Brice an excuse for a further delay. A linesman ran onto the field and put the ball back a further yard. Legitimate time-wasting! As Brice shaped to take the kick, opposing centre forward Max Murray danced about in front of the ball. Yet again, this was an instance of a Rangers player assisting Ayr United to waste time. The game could not proceed until Murray had been ushered back the necessary ten yards from the ball. Brice then took the time to place the ball yet again before hitting it from his own penalty area to the Rangers penalty area at the Somerset Road end. It was met by Scotland captain George Young, who made a poor attempt at a headed clearance, and the ball fell to Ayr winger Willie Japp, who hared in on goal. Goalkeeper George Niven had already dived by the time Japp was drawing back his foot to drive the ball into the net. Japp then got into a fankle and struck the ball with his heel rather than his instep. In effect, it was a complete miskick, and the Ayr winger was so angry with himself that he turned away in disgust. It was a routine ball for Niven, even although he was on the ground. Or, rather, it should have been a routine ball. What happened next defied belief. The ball struck a hard patch of mud before soaring upwards and over the goalkeeper into the net. The ball truly took an erratic course for what remains the most famous miskicked goal in the history of Ayr United. It was a fantastic piece of luck. The home fans were hysterical, and a report that 'Japp and Price almost jumped over the crossbar in their excitement' indicated that at least one journalist was in a similar frame of mind.

Only one factor tempered the excitement. There was the matter of the nine minutes which still had to be played. Watches were anxiously consulted and corner-kicks were just as anxiously repelled during these closing minutes. The final whistle was sweet music.

Ayr United: Travers, Paterson, Thomson, Traynor, Brice, Telfer, Japp. Paton, Price, Whittle and McMillan.

Rangers: Niven, Shearer, Caldow, McColl, Young, Davis, Scott, Simpson, Murray, Baird and Hubbard.

Hamilton Accies v. Ayr United

29 March 1958
Douglas Park

Scottish League Second Division

If the story of this game appeared in comic fiction, it would be rejected as far-fetched nonsense. Yet readers can be assured that what they are about to read did actually happen. In the interests of accuracy, three match reports were closely examined to authenticate details which stretch credibility.

With both clubs out of the promotion chase, there was nothing to suggest that this game would be anything other than ordinary. However, the 1957/58 season did see Ayr United both score and concede a large number of goals. The final table showed ninety-eight scored for the loss of eighty-one. This correctly implies that there were some colourful scorelines; such as a 7-4 home win over Forfar Athletic and a 6-5 defeat away to Cowdenbeath. There was, therefore, evidence that Ayr United were capable of scoring and conceding a higher-than-average amount of goals in the same match.

The scoring action began after three minutes had been played. Willie Bradley connected with a corner-kick from the right and drove the ball past Samson in the Accies goal. In striving for an equaliser, former Ayr United centre forward Guy Lennox proved to be a troublesome opponent. Ayr goalkeeper Jim Fulton did well to divert a Lennox effort for a corner-kick and, in a subsequent attack, the latter did get the ball in the net, but was justly denied by an offside decision.

The Accies maintained their attacking strategy with the result that Ayr United rarely threatened at this stage. It was consistent with the run of play when McLean advanced on Fulton's goal to equalise with thirty-seven minutes played. A half-time scoreline of 1-1 would have been relatively satisfactory and it was almost achieved. In the final minute of the first half, Ayr full-back Alex Paterson chopped down Hastings at the cost of a penalty kick, which Richmond scored from.

Having scored within a minute of one side of the break, the home team then managed to score within a minute of the other side of the break. Although the ball was deflected past Jim Fulton by John Telfer, it was not diverted from its path sufficiently to be recorded as an own goal and it was credited to Anderson. When, after fifty-three minutes, Guy Lennox headed his team 4-1 in front, it was all looking a bit bleak.

Entering the last twenty minutes, the 4-1 scoreline still persisted. Yet it was noticeable that the game continued to be played at a fast pace. This was indicative that Ayr United had not yet lost interest. Adam Haugh hit what looked like a hopeful lob in the direction of the Hamilton goal. It was met by Peter Price, who hit it on the drop to score. Time seventy-two minutes; score 4-2. The same end was soon revisited, and Price met a cross from the right to head it past Samson. Time seventy-three minutes; score 4-3. Home winger Agnew missed a great chance when clear, and his team was soon punished for that miss. Sam McMillan released Price to score. Time seventy-eight minutes; score 4-4. These were sensational developments, and the scale of the sensation was on the brink of escalating. Alex Paterson took a free-kick, which fell for Price to tap home. Time eighty minutes; score 4-5.

In order to comprehend the magnitude of this, it would be worthwhile recapping. Hamilton Accies were winning 4-1 until Peter Price scored four goals in eight minutes to put Ayr United in front. Up until then, he had scarcely been involved. Perhaps the Hamilton defenders had been lured into a false sense of security.

Of course, ten more minutes still needed to be played, but that time remained scoreless. It made for a fantastic story on an even more fantastic scoring feat.

Hamilton Accies 4
McLean, Richmond, Anderson
Lennox

Ayr United 5
Bradley, Price (4)

League Goals 1957/58	
Price	46
A. McIntyre	16
McMillan	10
Fulton	6
Bradley	5
Whittle	5
Stevenson	4
Hendry	1
Paton	1
'Junior'	1
Traynor	1
Craig (Dumbarton)	1 own goal
Duncan (Cowdenbeath)	1 own goal
Total	**98**

Peter Price, Ayr United's most prolific goalscorer of all time.

Peter Price scored fifty-four competitive goals for Ayr United that season; forty-six of them were in the League. That nothing better than fifth place was achieved was clearly down to the trend of scoring goals and losing them almost in equal measure.

P	W	D	L	F	A	Points
36	18	6	12	98	81	42

Hamilton Accies: Samson, McCabe, Young, Strickland, Richmond, Walker, Agnew, McLean, Lennox, Anderson and Hastings.
Ayr United: J. Fulton, Paterson, Telfer, W. McIntyre, Hannah, Haugh, A. McIntyre, McMillan, Price, W. Fulton and Bradley.

Ayr United v. Motherwell

12 September 1959   Scottish League First Division
Somerset Park

Bobby Ancell, the Motherwell manager, earnestly believed in giving young players a chance. He once refused to ask for the postponement of a Motherwell v. Dundee United game, even although he had three players away on international duty. He drafted in five reserve players, three of whom were aged seventeen, and his team won. The nickname 'Ancell's Babes' emerged in view of the young players whom he regularly selected. Ian St John was the brightest of these 'babes'. In the season before this game at Ayr, he had scored thirty-one competitive goals, and he was destined to score an identical number in 1959/60. Four weeks earlier, he had scored a hat-trick in the space of two-and-a-half minutes, against Hibs at Easter Road in a League Cup sectional tie. Motherwell took full points in that section, despite the inclusion of Rangers. The message was clear: Motherwell were a quality team in which St John, in particular, would require watching closely. There was also an element of experience in the side. Jim Forrest and Charlie Aitken had both been at Fir Park since 1949.

Manager Jacky Cox succeeded in getting his Ayr players into a good frame of mind; so much so, that an attacking strategy was adopted from the start. It brought an early reward. Willie Paton fed the ball to Peter Price, who wrong-footed the visiting defence with a clever back-heel. Team-mates Sam McMillan and Willie Paton then converged on the ball at the same time. Paton had the presence of mind to ease up in order to allow McMillan to score. With just five minutes played, it was a fabulous start.

Ayr United assumed control for most of the first half. Centre-half Jim McLean negated the threat of St John, and behind him, goalkeeper Ian Hamilton was rock solid. Willie McIntyre prevented Pat Quinn and Bobby Roberts from making an impact. John Paterson did likewise with Willie Hunter, whom Bobby Ancell claimed was the most skilled of his 'babes'. Yet there was a lot more to the Ayr United game-plan than merely setting out to stifle the opposition. Up front, Peter Price gave John Martis a torrid time.

Five minutes before half-time, Charlie Aitken attempted a clearance by way of an overhead kick. It was an ineffective clearance, which fell to Jim McGhee, who crossed for Sam McMillan to nod the ball in the direction of Peter Price, who placed it past Hastie Weir. At 2-0, there might have been a tendency to play out time until the interval, but that notion was resisted. Just a minute after that goal, Price and Martis got caught up in a challenge for possession. It was a challenge which only Price was going to win. After doing so, he put the ball out via the foot of a post – beaten by inches!

At the outset of the second half, Motherwell looked set on making amends as quickly as possible. A fantastic drive from Pat Quinn struck the underside of the crossbar, and Bobby Roberts reacted first. The lead was now fragile at 2-1. Encouraged by this success, the visitors maintained an attacking initiative, but it was to little avail. As in the first half, each threat was countered, and the Ayr United defenders grew in stature in the process.

Twenty minutes were left when McCallum, the visiting left-back, made a hashed clearance which was picked up by Billy Fulton. Fulton then dribbled the ball towards the middle, before parting with it to Price, whose shot at goal was stopped by Jim McGhee, who promptly slammed it home. Within a minute, Price seized onto a long ball, beat Martis then shot Ayr United 4-1 ahead. Few had considered the team to have a chance of overturning the challenge of the much-fancied Motherwell side. However, the best goal of the game had yet to come. In the seventy-ninth minute, McGhee broke through from midfield then parted with

---

Ayr United 5   **Motherwell 2**
McMillan, Price (3), McGhee   *Roberts, Hunter*

League Goals 1959/60	
Price	17
McGhee	15
McMillan	10
W. McIntyre	8
Fulton	7
Paton	3
McGuinness	2
Elliot	1
A. McIntyre	1
Telfer	1
Total	**65**

the ball to Price, who was situated at the edge of the penalty area. Hastie Weir emerged from his goal in an attempt to close down the Ayr striker. To his credit, Weir saved the thunderous shot which came his way, but the inevitable was merely delayed. From the rebound, a quality header sealed a Peter Price hat-trick. At 5-1 up against such illustrious opponents, the fans roared excitedly. Willie Hunter did manage to score a second goal for Motherwell, although it did not detract from a performance which earned a great ovation at the end.

At half-time, it had been feared that the pace would tell on Ayr United in the second half, but it was a groundless fear. The punishing speed of the game was maintained in that period, yet it seemed to have more of an adverse effect on Motherwell. With some luck, the scoreline could have reached even greater proportions. Peter Price was able to look back on a well-taken hat-trick, but he was further able to reflect on putting the ball in the net twice more, only to be frustrated by offside awards.

Ayr United: Hamilton, Burn, Paterson, W. McIntyre, McLean, Elliot, Fulton, McMillan, Price, Paton and McGhee.
Motherwell: Weir, Forrest, McCallum, Aitken, Martis, McCann, Hunter, Reid, St John, Quinn and Roberts.

Rangers v. Ayr United

19 September 1959
Ibrox Park

Scottish League First Division

A fortnight before this match, Ayr United also turned up in Glasgow on First Division duty. The outcome was a miserable performance, which ended in a 5-0 debacle against Third Lanark at Cathkin Park. It brought forth a newspaper comment that stated: 'Ayr are certainly not in pace with the Division One regulars'. Yet it was premature to be too critical. It was, after all, just the second League fixture of the season. This, of course, begs the question of what happened in the League opener. That result was Ayr United 1 Clyde 2. Such form was also reflected in a failure to qualify from a League Cup section in opposition to Falkirk, Hamilton Accies and Berwick Rangers. After having won the Second Division title in such cavalier style, the going proved to be tough until the Motherwell match mentioned previously. Had Ayr United finally found some momentum, or had the Motherwell game represented one of those mad days when things just happen to go right? The answer was to come in a more emphatic way than anyone could have dreamt.

The expression 'showboating' had not yet been thought of in a football context. Yet there were incidents in this game at Ibrox, which suggested that such a description would have been most fitting in the context of Ayr United's performance. In the real olden days, the expression 'gallery work' might have been used. Here, in 1959, it was probably just known as 'showing off'. Let's just get to the point and state that Ayr United won in style.

In the early stages, the balance of play favoured Ayr United. If there was any trepidation about playing on the ground of the reigning League Champions, it was not apparent. Reputations were not respected, and when the lead was taken in the sixteenth minute, it was fully deserved. On the left edge of the penalty area, Peter Price picked up possession and squared it to Dan McGuinness, who was immediately tackled by Little but still managed to lay the ball off to Jim McGhee. Initially, McGhee looked to have overrun the ball. He quickly corrected the situation before beating George Niven with a low shot.

Not content with this, the Ayr forwards were soon buzzing around Niven's goal again. In time, this enterprise paid off. Willie Paton, playing against his former club, initiated a move with Sam McMillan. The move culminated in Price setting up McGhee to drive the ball high into the Rangers net. To lead 2-0 at Ibrox was a highly satisfactory situation, yet still the goal lust was not fully satisfied. In the forty-fourth minute, McGhee sent the ball across the face of goal. It was picked up by Price, who had strayed onto the right wing. Price eased past Telfer, then cut it back towards Dan McGuinness, who was advancing on goal. Having been signed in the summer from Johnstone Burgh, McGuinness did not possess much in the way of big-match experience. It therefore almost beggared belief when he attempted to sell the Rangers defence a dummy – which they bought! He purposely let the ball go through his legs to the better placed Billy Elliot, who fired it into the net.

Meanwhile, at Somerset Park, the spectators at the reserve game were treated to a loudspeaker announcement declaring a half-time score of Rangers 0 Ayr United 3. At the end of 1959/60, Rangers were able to reflect on having easily the best defensive record in the Scottish Leagues but, in this match, the reputation of the famous 'Iron Curtain' was in tatters. Within five minutes of the start of the second half, George Niven had pulled off a great save from a Jim McGhee drive and Peter Price had struck the crossbar with a header. This indicated the possibility of an even greater rout, although it did not materialise. Ayr United gradually resorted to soaking up the home attacks which had a desperate look about them.

Rangers 0

Ayr United 3
McGhee (2), Elliot

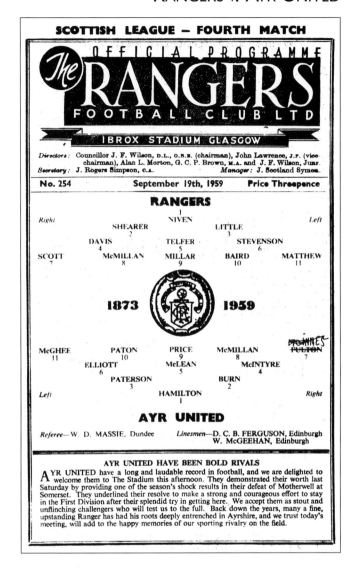

RANGERS

| | 1 | |
| | NIVEN | |
Right | SHEARER | LITTLE | Left
2	3	
DAVIS	TELFER	STEVENSON
4	5	6
SCOTT | McMILLAN | MILLAR | BAIRD | MATTHEW
7 | 8 | 9 | 10 | 11

1873   1959

McGHEE | PATON | PRICE | McMILLAN | ~~McINNES~~ FULTON
11 | 10 | 9 | 8 | 7
ELLIOTT	McLEAN	McINTYRE
6	5	4
PATERSON	BURN
3	2
Left	HAMILTON		Right
1

AYR UNITED

Referee—W. D. MASSIE, Dundee   *Linesmen*—D. C. B. FERGUSON, Edinburgh
W. McGEEHAN, Edinburgh

AYR UNITED HAVE BEEN BOLD RIVALS

AYR UNITED have a long and laudable record in football, and we are delighted to welcome them to The Stadium this afternoon. They demonstrated their worth last Saturday by providing one of the season's shock results in their defeat of Motherwell at Somerset. They underlined their resolve to make a strong and courageous effort to stay in the First Division after their splendid try in getting here. We accept them as stout and unflinching challengers who will test us to the full. Back down the years, many a fine, upstanding Ranger has had his roots deeply entrenched in Ayrshire, and we trust today's meeting, will add to the happy memories of our sporting rivalry on the field.

Their superiority continued to be asserted, but it was just done in different ways. A prime example came when Sam McMillan was being challenged by Stevenson. In an act of contempt, he bent down and adjusted his stocking, while the ball was still at his feet. It must have been demoralising to the Rangers man and his team-mates. Even this level of superiority did not translate itself into further goals, not that there were any complaints. A 3-0 victory was more than satisfactory. Only the more mature fans were able to recall the previous Ayr United victory at Ibrox. That occasion, also covered in this book, had been as far back as February 1915.

Rangers: Niven, Shearer, Little, Davis, Telfer, Stevenson, Scott, McMillan, Millar, Baird and Matthew.
Ayr United: Hamilton, Burn, Paterson, W. McIntyre, McLean, Elliot, McGuinness, McMillan, Price, Paton and McGhee.

CELTIC v. AYR UNITED

7 November 1959   Scottish League First Division
Celtic Park

'A statistician delving into the records with a number nine shovel won't be able to dig up an occasion when Ayr United beat both Rangers and Celtic away from home in the same season.' These words were attributable to Bill Hannah, who wrote in the *Ayr Advertiser* under the pen name Carrick Hill. In later years, a calling into the ministry caused Bill's career path to alter, but he continued to have the same intense feelings for Ayr United. His initial career in journalism, allied to his love of the club, enabled him to write reports which beautifully encapsulated the type of emotion felt by genuine supporters.

Prior to this match, Peter Price had barely slept over a period of three days. This was due to his wife, Christina, being in hospital for the impending birth of a baby girl called Jacqueline (6lb 10oz). With typical resolve, the small matter of tiredness was never going to prevent him from taking the field at Celtic Park.

Jacky Cox had to contemplate how he was going to replace centre-half Jim McLean, injured the week before at Airdrie. The problem was solved by switching John Paterson from his regular left-back position – it was fortunate that he had played as a centre-half while with Hibs. George McIntyre came in at left-back to fill the void left by Paterson.

It was evident early on that this match would contain goals. There was little time for the subtlety of midfield creation, as either one goal or the other withstood pressure. With thirty minutes played, something inevitably gave. Bertie Peacock made a poor clearance, which was picked up by Willie McIntyre. In turn, McIntyre passed to Billy Elliot, who fed the ball to Sam McMillan. McMillan then dashed past Bobby Evans, before beating John Fallon in the Celtic goal. At half-time, Ayr United were still in front by that single goal.

It would reasonably have been expected that Celtic would chase the game in the early stages of the second half, but this expectation was turned on its head in the opening minutes after the restart. Bobby Evans fouled Peter Price in dangerously close proximity to the Celtic penalty area. From the resultant free-kick, Jim McGhee saw his effort deflected by left-back Donnelly. It was a fortuitous deflection because the ball landed nicely for Sam McMillan, who put Ayr United 2-0 up.

In the late 1950s and early '60s, there was a theory that Ayr United struggled whenever called upon to play under floodlights. There was evidence to support the theory. The descending gloom caused the Celtic Park lights to be switched on. Whether coincidentally, or not, the home fans began to roar their team on at a higher decibel level. In the sixty-first minute, a well-struck drive from Bertie Auld found its way past Ian Hamilton. Six minutes after that, Celtic equalised. Stevie Chalmers hit a shot which John Divers got a boot to and diverted it in. (One report called it a 'mishit'.) Yet, by any definition, the score was now 2-2. Three weeks after this game, Ayr United were to lose 4-3 away to St Mirren after blowing a lead when the floodlights went on. This added further emphasis to the argument about Ayr United having difficulty in coping under floodlights.

As the game progressed, Celtic did succeed in winning corner-kicks, but they were all fruitless. In the eighty-fourth minute, a corner-kick at the other end brought a spectacular development. It was taken by Jim 'Tottie' McGhee, who crossed the ball into a busy penalty area. It swerved in past the near post, and John Fallon was unable to grasp it cleanly, thereby allowing it to continue on its flight towards the back of the Celtic net.

'Tottie' McGhee's winner, directly from a corner-kick, became a part of local footballing

---

Celtic 2   **Ayr United 3**
Auld, Divers   *McMillan (2), McGhee*

CELTIC

Official **Programme**

JOHN COLRAIN

SCOTTISH LEAGUE—DIV. 1

CELTIC v. AYR UNITED

Saturday, 7th November, 1959

Kick-off 3 p.m.

No. 7

PRICE THREEPENCE

legend, although the story of it was embellished slightly in later years. The embellishment related to the goal time. It was commonly told that it came in the last minute or, in extreme cases, with the last kick of the match.

Although the victory at Celtic Park was considered to be in the 'shock result' category, this may have been an overstatement when it is considered that the completed First Division table of 1959/60 shows that Ayr United finished above Celtic.

Celtic: Fallon, Mackay, Donnelly, Smith, Evans, Peacock, Chalmers, Jackson, Colrain, Divers and Auld.

Ayr United: Hamilton, Burn, G. McIntyre, W. McIntyre, Paterson, Elliot, Fulton, McMillan, Price, Paton and McGhee.

AYR UNITED v. RANGERS

24 December 1960   Scottish League First Division
Somerset Park

The completed First Division table from the 1960/61 season shows Ayr United and Rangers to be separated by its entire length, with a points gap of twenty-nine (at *two* points for a win). In the context of the season before, this was a bitter disappointment. Supporters struggled to understand how the club could go into such rapid decline; although the decline was to accelerate ever more rapidly in the years ahead. The prospect of a Christmas Eve visit from Rangers was far from a cheery one. This match was entered with just one point having been taken from the previous eight League fixtures. Jacky Cox strove hard in pursuit of a solution. During that dismal run, one of his changes was to introduce John Gallacher, a young goalkeeper whom he had signed from Benburb in the summer. Prior to facing Rangers, he had made just three first-team appearances. Two days before the match, Davie Curlett, formerly with Kilmarnock, was signed from Dundee. He went straight into the team and wore the shirt which would otherwise have been worn by Sam McMillan, who had suffered an injury at Tannadice on the previous Saturday.

Up to this point of the season, Ayr United had only numbered one victory in the League Cup and League matches played. That win had been against Hearts on 15 October, when Billy Fulton had scored the only goal of the game against the reigning League Champions. Would it again be possible for the Ayr players to raise their game in the face of fancied opposition?

At the outset, the Rangers players were closed down at every opportunity. Man-to-man marking was strict, and it had to be to contain the potential threat. In particular, Jim McLean worked very hard to deny space to striker Jimmy Millar. The policy of containment worked until the nineteenth minute, when Bobby Walker tripped Davie Wilson. Referee Stewart pointed to the penalty spot for a decision which was beyond dispute, however regrettable it might have been. The next development has since been retold to succeeding generations of Ayr United supporters. It was a Rangers team full of household names, and the responsiblity for the penalty kick was delegated to Ralph Brand. A hush descended over Somerset Park, then Brand hit a shot which was on course for the roof of the net, but John Gallacher rose sufficiently to get a hand to it. In spectacular fashion, he touched the ball over the crossbar for a fruitless corner-kick. It was an inspired save, which belied his age and inexperience. His inspiration did not desert him. Minutes later, he dived at the feet of Brand to thwart a dangerous situation. Further danger was visited on the Ayr goal when an Alex Scott cross landed in the vicinity of Millar. Luckily, he miskicked.

In the twenty-eighth minute, Davie Curlett supplied Billy Fulton with the ball. Fulton then cleverly threaded it between Rangers defenders Shearer and Paterson. It therefore reached the intended recipient, Peter Price. Price then sped away from the aforementioned Rangers players and, from marginally inside the penalty area, he delivered a firmly-struck low shot, which beat goalkeeper George Niven. The joy of this goal manifested itself in cheers that would have been heard a considerable distance from the ground. Alastair McIntyre squandered a good chance to increase the lead when he shot too high from inside the six-yard box.

Early in the second half, Bobby Thomson kept the lead intact by heading off the line with Gallacher beaten. At the other end, Ramsay Burn attempted a forty-yard lob, which Niven did well to touch over the crossbar. However, from this point on, Rangers did the bulk of the

---

Ayr United 1   **Rangers 0**
Price

3D   3D

AYR UNITED FOOTBALL AND ATHLETIC CLUB

Official Programme
1960-61

SATURDAY, 24th DECEMBER
Kick-off 2.15 p.m.

Scottish League - First Division

AYR UNITED
versus
RANGERS

3D   Lucky N°   2802   3D

The programme number indicates long odds in the prize draw.

attacking. Threatening crosses and numerous corner-kicks rained in on the Ayr goal. Yet Gallacher was determined to keep a clean sheet and his form remained impeccable.

Tension began to mount. Alastair McIntyre was lectured for a foul on Jim Baxter. In terms of menace, this foul was soon eclipsed by Harold Davis. His tackle on Ayr's Jim McGhee tended more towards vicious than menacing. Davis had a reputation as a hard man, yet his motivation here was almost certainly born out of frustration. Mr Stewart was soon delivering another warning. This time, the offender was Bobby Thomson, who had bundled Davis out of possession.

In the last fifteen minutes, the Ayr United game plan was not flamboyant. The defending became increasingly desperate. Even the forwards had to lie deep in order to help block out the constant crosses and shots. At last, the final whistle was blown, and it signalled a pitch invasion of overjoyed fans.

In September 1993, a letter from Sweden arrived at Somerset Park. In it, the writer described in the following terms, precisely how he had developed an interest in Ayr United.

'At Christmas time, the pools used to take a week's break but, for reasons unknown to me, the pools company decided that on Christmas Eve, 1960, there would be a coupon, not with English matches, because they didn't play that Saturday, but with Scottish matches. Oh boy! Match one was Ayr United (last in the table) at home to mighty Glasgow Rangers, miles ahead at the top. How easy it seemed to be. People looked at the League table and marked for an away win. Then, when we were eating our Christmas Eve supper, we turned on the radio to hear the results – match one: Ayr United 1 Rangers 0. Home win. Yes, so it was. An hour later we put on the news again, and they repeated the result. We hadn't heard wrong. When all the coupons in the whole of Sweden had been checked the following Wednesday, there was not a single person who had got all twelve matches right. 98 per cent had got the Ayr v. Rangers result wrong, and those who had got that one right had failed to put one or two other results right instead. That week, around 28/29 December 1960, I decided to take a close interest in Ayr United – the club that had turned not only Rangers, but every pools expert in Sweden inside out, and ever since that day, the Ayr result is the first I am looking for when I turn on the radio on Saturday afternoons (BBC World Service) or open my Sunday newspaper to read the football results. As with all clubs, there have been ups and downs, as there will continue to be, but I will always keep on supporting Ayr United Football Club of Scotland more than any other club in the world.'

The letter was signed by one Lars-Olof Wendler.

Ayr United: Gallacher, Burn, Thomson, Walker, McLean, Glen, A. McIntyre, Curlett, Price, Fulton and McGhee.

Rangers: Niven, Shearer, Caldow, Davis, Paterson, Baxter, Scott, McMillan, Millar, Brand and Wilson.

ABERDEEN v. AYR UNITED

15 February 1964   Scottish Cup Third Round
Pittodrie

It was not even remotely considered that Ayr United might win this tie. 1964 remains the blackest year in the history of the club. In November of that year, the *Sunday Express* ran a story about the imminent closure of the club. The basis of the story was that the ground would be sold off to clear the outstanding debts. Horrifyingly, the *Sunday Express* was correct with regard to the intentions, but the directors ensured that the club would continue for a time which was dependent on 'the support it receives from the public of Ayr and district through the turnstiles and the development club'. A takeover managed to avert the crisis.

It was a crisis which had begun fermenting earlier in the year when the club travelled to Aberdeen for this Scottish Cup tie. The Aberdeen match programme was riddled with inaccuracies, but the reference to Ayr United being fourth from bottom of the Second Division was correct. In accordance with the League format at that time, this meant that Ayr United had the fourth worst team in Scotland. History was also against the club. The previous Scottish Cup meeting between the clubs had taken place at Pittodrie in 1947. It had been the occasion of an 8-0 Aberdeen win, and the programme cover for the 1964 tie carried a photograph of the final goal in that particular demise. In addition, there was no historical precedent for Ayr United having an away Scottish Cup win against a club from a higher League. In a later age, the task being faced would have been described as 'damage limitation'.

The first-half pattern was consistent with expectations. Even breaking into the Aberdeen half proved to be impossible for long stretches. That the home team had difficulty in scoring was, at times, caused by them having too many players in forward positions. It seemed that the home half-backs just could not resist the opportunity to help their forwards. At least, that was the intention. They hindered rather than helped.

At the heart of the Ayr defence, Willie Toner, a former international, called on all his reserves of experience. Full-back John Murphy currently holds the club record for appearances, but, here in 1964, he was in his first senior season, as was fellow full-back Eddie Maxwell. This inexperience did not prevent them from getting the measure of wingers Kerrigan and Hume. Wing-halves Billy Frew and Jim Lindsay had to drop back to help repel the consistent onslaught. Behind them, goalkeeper John Gallacher was in brilliant form. The tactics were blindingly simple. They revolved around getting players behind the ball and clearing it as far as possible whenever the opportunity arose.

There was an abundance of fraught moments. For example, Charlie Cooke crossed for Ernie Winchester to effect a diving header, which Gallacher saved right at the post. At the other end, it took until seconds from the interval for Ayr United to get a chance at goal. Kenny Cunningham fared no better than shooting into the side netting.

With the second half ten minutes old, the expected happened. Smith crossed for Graham to score with a left-foot shot, which entered the net via a post. With Aberdeen a goal up, it was further expected that this would cause a settling down which would lead to further scoring. It so nearly went according to the script. John Gallacher made a superlative double-save from Cooke and Winchester to maintain the slender deficit.

In the seventy-seventh minute, Johnny Hubbard sent in a cross, which was dropped by John 'Tubby' Ogston in the Aberdeen goal. Sam McMillan seized on the loose ball and laid it off to Kenny Cunningham who equalised. 1-1 at an advanced stage of the game! It defied belief.

Aberdeen 1   **Ayr United 2**
Graham   *Cunningham*
                                        Kilgannon

ABERDEEN v. AYR UNITED

Our flashback picture from the 1947 cup-tie shows George Hamilton scoring the Dons' eighth goal. McNeil, the Ayr right back, is making a vain effort to intercept the ball.

As the tie reached the closing minutes, a Somerset Park replay was looking like a possibility. By then it was a battle against the clock. Three minutes remained when John Gallacher made a long downfield clearance, which struck centre-half Coutts on the shoulder. The ball then fell nicely to Ayr striker Johnny Kilgannon, who instantly rounded Coutts and ran in on the advancing Ogston. Kilgannon hit a shot which was far from crisp, yet the ball still rose over Ogston and dipped into the net. Aberdeen 1 Ayr United 2 with eighty-seven minutes on the clock – was this really happening?

Of course, there were still several minutes left for Aberdeen to make a desperate attempt at salvaging the tie. The nearest they came was when Doug Coutts went up for a corner-kick and got in a header which went inches wide of the Ayr goal. Time was then called on a marvellous tactical victory for manager Bobby Flavell, who had known the team's limitations and planned accordingly. The author will forever remember the boyhood thrill of seeing the result being spelled out on the BBC teleprinter.

This put Ayr United into the quarter-finals, which involved an away tie against Dunfermline Athletic. So what happened at Dunfermline? The answer is that Ayr United found their true 1964 form and lost 7-0.

Aberdeen: Ogston, Shewan, Hogg, Burns, Coutts, Smith, Kerrigan, Cooke, Graham, Winchester and Hume.

Ayr United: Gallacher, Murphy, Maxwell, Frew, Toner, Lindsay, Hubbard, McMillan, Kilgannon, Grant and Cunningham.

KILMARNOCK v. AYR UNITED

26 April 1965   Ayrshire Cup Final
Rugby Park

How can an Ayrshire Cup game be worthy of inclusion in a book of classic matches? In the nineteenth century, the Ayrshire Cup was a much coveted trophy. In order to convey the importance of the competition, it is worth mentioning that, in season 1880/81, fifty-three names were in the first-round draw. It gradually diminished in importance to the extent that only Ayr United and Kilmarnock competed. In effect, every match became a final. However, the lifting of such a handsome trophy was a lesser consideration than outdoing a county rival. Ayrshire Cup ties do not remotely come under the definition of competitive matches, even though they were, in their own way. The circumstances in 1965, were though, sufficiently different to justify inclusion.

On the Saturday prior to this Monday evening match, Kilmarnock had beaten Hearts 2-0 at Tynecastle Park. That result had clinched the League Championship for Kilmarnock on goal average. On the same afternoon, Ayr United had beaten Stranraer 2-0 at Somerset Park in the club's penultimate League fixture of the 1964/65 season. Nevertheless, the completed tables showed Ayr United to be second from the foot of the Second Division: a placing which caused the embarrassment of having to apply for re-election. This meant that the Ayrshire Cup final of 1965 comprised a meeting between the country's highest-placed club and the second lowest. It was just a quirk of fate that Killie's best ever season coincided with Ayr United's worst.

Before the kick-off, Kilmarnock did a lap of honour with the Championship trophy. Understandably, this was done to tremendous acclaim. They then lined up with the same team which had pulled off the memorable win against Hearts. A daunting prospect indeed!

A torrential downpour greeted the kick-off. It was perhaps symbolic of the anticipated downpour on the Ayr goal and that was exactly what materialised. Alastair Paton, in the Ayr goal, was quickly called into action. Attack after attack indicated that a very one-sided game was in prospect, but the home team had no material reward to show for this supremacy. Bertie Black went close with a fine drive before Kilmarnock suffered the handicap of losing Jacky McInally with a head injury. Ten minutes later he returned to the fray.

The Ayr team did manage to muster some spirited attacks, yet these were brief forays. At the other end, Sneddon and Black both had shots which were bound for the Ayr net. The respective shots were frantically blocked. In a similar fashion, crosses from Tommy McLean and Hugh McIlroy were cleared with equal lack of ceremony. Neither was there anything refined about much of the tackling by the Ayr defenders. This resulted in Eddie Monan being booked and some of his team-mates being warned.

In the thirty-first minute, there was a quite sensational development when Ayr winger Davie Paterson fired the ball into the Kilmarnock net from thirty yards. Still, there was the considerable matter of the amount of time left. Yet it almost became 2-0 several minutes later. It was just unfortunate that Charlie Oliphant missed the great chance presented to him. In the thirty-seventh minute, an even greater chance was presented to Alex McAnespie after Davie Paterson had been fouled in the box. 'Sanny' took the resultant penalty-kick only to be denied by a Bobby Ferguson save. He nearly atoned when he got his head to the rebound, but Ferguson saved that too.

In the second half, Kilmarnock again failed to produce the standard of football which had won them the title, although this was not due to a lack of application. Determined efforts to

---

Kilmarnock 0   **Ayr United 1**
D. Paterson

KILMARNOCK v. AYR UNITED

Above: 1964/65 may have been traumatic but the team atoned a season later. This squad photograph was taken in the early part of 1965/66. From left to right, back row: Oliphant, Millar, Monan, Malone, McAnespie, Murphy, Paton. Front row: Grant, McMillan, Cockburn, Hawkshaw, Paterson.

Left: John Paton, Tom McGawn and Lewis Thow. These three directors, along with Malcolm McPhail and Bob McCall, rescued Ayr United from extinction during 1964/65.

get an equalising goal were met by even more determined efforts to keep them out. The defending remained desperate. However, the match took an unexpected twist in the closing minutes when Ayr United applied some attacking pressure. The final whistle heralded the most unlikely of results.

After enduring the worst League campaign in the club's history, there were only two significant signings in the summer of 1965. These players were winger Johnny Grant and inside forward Ian Hawkshaw. For the most part, the players who had struggled so badly were entrusted with carrying the club into 1965/66. The confidence enrusted in these players was rewarded with the Second Division Championship at the end of that season.

Kilmarnock: Ferguson, King, Watson, Murray, McGrory, Beattie, McLean, McInally, Black, Sneddon and McIlroy.

Ayr United: Paton, Malone, Murphy, Thomson, Monan, McAnespie, D. Paterson, McMillan, Oliphant, Kerr and A. Paterson.

30 August 1969
Somerset Park

Scottish League First Division

After winning the Second Division Championship in 1966, Ayr United endured a brief and miserable sojourn in top-flight football. The word 'endured' is most apt. At one stage of that 1966/67 season, one solitary point was taken over the course of fifteen consecutive League fixtures. Two seasons in the Second Division followed, culminating in promotion again in 1969. It was not an especially glorious promotion. The gap from champions Motherwell extended to eleven points; fairly substantial, on the basis of two points for a win. Further diluting the sense of euphoria was the fact that promotion was clinched on the day of an away defeat against Queen of the South. On the return journey, car radios relayed the news that Ayr United had made it by virtue of Stirling Albion and East Fife also losing. This prompted some to stop at Thornhill for a swift, or not so swift, half!

The opening First Division fixture of 1969/70 brought Hibs to Somerset Park. Ayr United had just won a League Cup section including Queen of the South, East Stirling and Queen's Park. This was the season in which goal difference replaced goal average to separate teams tied on points and the section had been won by this means. In summary, there was nothing to suggest that a Hibs team riddled with household names could be beaten. Apart, of course, from the infectious enthusiasm and optimism of manager Ally MacLeod. He had the ability to instill an enormous amount of self-belief into his part-time players.

On a gloriously sunny afternoon, Ayr United set about attacking the railway end in the first half. It was immediately obvious that there was a feeling of inspiration about the team. This attitude brought a return in the thirteenth minute. Cutty Young played the ball back to Dick Malone, who sent over a cross which seemed to hang in the air. Alex Ingram, ever menacing in the air, won the ball and headed it down to Jacky Ferguson, who shot it under Gordon Marshall, much to the elation of the crowd.

It was too early to pursue a policy of containment, besides which the team was not content to sit on a 1-0 lead. Confidence escalated. In the twenty-fourth minute, a low cross from Cutty Young wreaked havoc and Bobby Rough was on hand to fire home the second goal. The sun was shining, both literally and metaphorically. Alas, it shone a little less brightly three minutes from half-time when Cutty Young became the victim of a coarse challenge from Joe McBride. His retaliation, though understandable, perhaps merited a booking. Referee Currie considered it to be worthy of a sending-off. An angry crowd voiced loudly their displeasure at the perceived injustice. Of more practical concern was the vulnerability of the 2-0 lead. To that point of the match, Cutty had torn at the Hibs defence with attacking abandon.

Ally MacLeod was not the type of person to cultivate negative thoughts. The early minutes of the second half even saw full-backs Dick Malone and John Murphy push forward in different raids. Admittedly there was a degree of caution, but, as the half progressed, it was refreshing to see that the team was far from impotent as an attacking force. With seventy-two minutes played, Davy McCulloch sent a fine pass to Bobby Rough, who fed the ball to Alex Ingram. When the latter parted with the ball, he did so into the back of the Hibs net. The space Dixie had been allowed was astonishing, and the errant Hibs defenders were punished for the lack of marking. Six minutes later, he had the ball in the net again. It was a pity that an earlier infringement caused the celebrations to be quickly stifled.

The 3-0 result was, in itself, special. To have achieved it with a man short for the whole second half was extra special. In the 1966/67 season, the club's first League win had come

---

Ayr United 3
Ingram, Ferguson, Rough

Hibs 0

Ayr United v. Hibs

Ayr United FC 1969/70. From left to right, back row: Jim McFadzean, Dick Malone, Davie Stewart, Rikki Fleming, Alec McAnespie, Dougie Mitchell, John Murphy. Front row: Sam McMillan (coach), Quintin Young, Tommy Reynolds, Jacky Ferguson, Neil Hood, Stan Quinn, Ally MacLeod (manager), Davie McCulloch, Bobby Rough, and Willie Wallace (trainer).

in the twenty-ninth fixture. To win the opening League game of 1969/70 was an indication that there would be no parallels with the horror of that previous First Division campaign.

On 13 December 1969, the clubs met at Easter Road in the return League fixture. The half-time score was 4-3 for Hibs, as was the full-time score. That result left Hibs on top of the First Division and they had fifteen goals in the 'goals against' column. Six of them had been scored by Ayr United.

Ayr United: Stewart, Malone, Murphy, Fleming, Quinn, Mitchell, Young, Ferguson, Ingram, McCulloch and Rough. *Substitute:* Hood.

Hibs: Marshall, Shevlane, Davis, Wilkinson, Black, Stanton, Marinello, Grant, McBride, Cormack and Stevenson. *Substitute:* O'Rourke.

AYR UNITED FOOTBALL CLUB

OFFICIAL PROGRAMME

6 D

SEASON 1969 - 70

SCOTTISH LEAGUE   FIRST DIVISION

HIBERNIAN

Saturday, 30th August

Kick-off 3 pm   N⁰. 143

Ayr United v. Rangers

13 September 1969
Somerset Park

Scottish League First Division
Attendance: 25,225

In the build-up to this match, it was correctly anticipated that there was going to be a large crowd. Traditionally, Rangers attract a vast support, even though relatively few have any affinity with the club's native Govan. The beautiful weather on the day of this match was further conducive to attracting a good crowd and, since entry was pay-at-the-gate, it was open to anyone who cared to turn up. Somerset Park was eventually transformed into a teeming mass of humanity. In total, 25,225 people passed through the turnstiles, whilst an unspecified number managed to clamber over walls or squeeze through narrow gaps to gain entry. A new ground record was set and it can never be beaten.

It was necessary for many spectators to sit or squat on the track; with the effect that photographs of the match had the illusion of there being no wall around the pitch. Compared to the wide open spaces of Ibrox Park, the Rangers players may have felt a sense of claustrophobia on taking to a field which was perilously near to being encroached upon. Before long, they would be feeling a far greater discomfort.

In the seventh minute, Bobby Rough crossed from the left and the ball landed at the feet of Cutty Young, who rounded full-back Mathieson with ease before sending a drive high into the Rangers net from twenty-five yards. The excitement was compounded by a further goal in the fourteenth minute. A Dick Malone cross was won by Alex Ingram, whose header into a space caused a chase between John Greig and Jacky Ferguson. The determination of Jacky Ferguson ensured that he got to the ball first and, in so doing, headed past Gerry Neef. 2-0 to Ayr United with less than a quarter of an hour played!

From this point onwards, Rangers carried no appreciable threat. In mentioning that the Ayr defence stood solid, it should not be interpreted that they retreated into a defensive shell. Cutty Young, a close-season signing from Kello Rovers, had belied his inexperience at this level, right from the start of the season. He was a difficult player to defend against because he had a natural repertoire of skills. Successive attacks brought forth different ways of beating defenders; each way was mesmeric. Rangers were therefore unable to concentrate solely on staging a fightback and had to play with the constant danger that Ayr United might score again.

The second half was entered with no further scoring having taken place. If anything about this day could have been described as mildly disappointing, it was the inability to kill the game off with a third goal. Alex Ingram broke clear but shot wide. Minutes later, Davie McCulloch might have scored, had he mustered more power on the shot. The lack of velocity allowed Gerry Neef to parry the shot then save it.

In midfield, Rikki Fleming epitomised class. Willie Johnston, in frustration, picked up a booking for fouling him. Ironically, Rikki Fleming had formerly been registered with Rangers.

In injury time, Colin Stein scored for Rangers, thereby creating a result with a false complexion of the true course of the game. A mass of Rangers supporters invaded the field in celebration when that goal was scored. Had it not crossed their minds that the resultant delay was potentially harmful to their own team? Obviously not! Yet so little time remained that it was probably a non-issue.

Never, before or since, has Somerset Park taken so long to empty. Right along the track, at the front of the stand, there was a long queue of people who shuffled towards the main gate. It was an unconventional exit route, but the circumstances were extraordinary.

Ayr United 2
Young, Ferguson

Rangers 1
Stein

Jacky Ferguson.

AYR UNITED v. RANGERS

AYR UNITED FOOTBALL CLUB

OFFICIAL PROGRAMME

6D··

SEASON 1969 - 70

SCOTTISH LEAGUE   FIRST DIVISION

RANGERS

Saturday, 13th September

Kick-off 3 pm   Nº 1491

To this day, Dougie Mitchell can relate an anecdote about something which was said when he and his Ayr United team-mates were leaving the field at the end. Jim Baxter came out with the line: 'Your bonus'll be a fish supper'.

It was a day memorable for the 2-1 victory, yet those of us who were there are more likely to reminisce about the crowd which overtaxed the capacity of the Somerset Park terracings. People still have clear recollections of the spot where they stood, sat or squatted that memorable day.

Ayr United: Stewart, Malone, Murphy, Fleming, Quinn, Mitchell, Young, Ferguson, Ingram, McCulloch and Rough. *Substitute:* McFadzean.

Rangers: Neef, Johansen, Mathieson, Greig, Provan, Baxter, Penman, Jardine, Stein, McDonald and Johnston. *Substitute:* Smith.

8 October 1969
Hampden Park

Scottish League Cup Semi-final
Attendance: 35,110

By this stage in the 1969/70 season, Ayr United were renowned for spirited displays of attacking football. Yet it was doubted whether such qualities would be sufficient to overthrow Celtic. Did a part-time team really stand a chance against opponents who would ultimately reach that season's European Cup final? With Ally MacLeod as manager, there had to be some kind of a chance. Ally was not a respecter of reputations and neither were his players. Hibs and Rangers had already been accounted for in the League and, on this occasion, the Ayr United line-up was the same. This was a team which was only altered when compelled to by utter necessity, such as injury or suspension. On the Wednesday evening of this tie, there was no need to contemplate what the likely team would be. It was the team which fans can still recite. Stewart, Malone, Murphy … the rest of it just flows from the tongue.

The quarter-final had not constituted a difficult passage. It involved a two-legged tie with Dumbarton. The first leg, at Boghead Park, was won 4-1 and the eventual 5-1 aggregate put the club onto a Hampden stage. This Ayr team had already proven what could be achieved within the relatively tight confines of Somerset Park, but the prospect of playing a major club at a large venue presented a potentially sterner test.

When the tie got underway, it became clear that Ayr United were not overawed by the occasion. Ally MacLeod would have had it no other way. This self-belief manifested itself with a goal in the thirty-second minute. A cross from Cutty Young saw Bobby Rough rise to it and head past John Fallon. The anticipated response materialised as Celtic chased in pursuit of a quick equaliser. Suitably stung, they responded by equalising before half-time. A hard-hit cross from Kenny Dalglish was diverted past Davie Stewart by the outstretched boot of John Hughes.

It is not known what Ally MacLeod said to his players at half-time, but it is not difficult to guess the gist of it. He would have praised his team to the hilt before sending them back out. Sadly, there was a threat to morale just five minutes after the resumption. Celtic were awarded a penalty after John Murphy had supposedly brought down Willie Wallace. Even the Glasgow-based press disputed the fairness of the award, a major concession in the 1960s. Tommy Gemmell squared the tie from the spot.

In the sixty-first minute, the injustice was corrected. Alex Ingram got involved in a tangle with Billy McNeill and the ball broke to Davie McCulloch, who ran on to shoot past Fallon. For much of the remainder of the statutory ninety minutes, Celtic lost their composure with an over-determination to avoid extra time. In a later age, this strategy would have been described as 'losing their shape'.

On moving into extra time, there was a sensational development in the fifth minute. Bobby Rough scored his second headed goal of the tie. There is no doubt that the Ayr United support would have included veterans of the 1950 semi-final, when a 3-2 lead was also held at an advanced stage. If that memory created lingering doubts, then these doubts proved to be justified. By half-time in extra time, Bertie Auld had made it 3-3 with a well-struck drive. Neither net was tested during the concluding portion of the tie.

The consequence of the result was a Hampden Park replay to be held the following Monday evening. The Ayr team was the same as in the original tie, even down to the listing of Neil Hood as a substitute. Everyone knew that it would be unaltered. The public

---

Ayr United 3
Rough (2), McCulloch

Celtic 3 (after extra time)
Hughes, Gemmell, Auld

Bobby Rough.

Stan Quinn.

imagination had been captivated to such an extent that the crowd at the replay soared to 47,831.

In the fourteenth minute of the rematch, a low drive from Bobby Rough was driven high into the Celtic net by Alex Ingram. From a Tommy Gemmell cross, Harry Hood headed his team level nine minutes later. Seven minutes into the second half, Stan Quinn's attempted clearance fell for Stevie Chalmers, who put Celtic 2-1 ahead. In the seventy-ninth minute, Alex Ingram connected with a low cross from Dougie Mitchell and the ball was destined for the back of the net until Ronnie Simpson made a diving save, after appearing to have been beaten. Simpson suffered a shoulder injury in the process and took no further part in the game. Perhaps through sympathy with the injured goalkeeper, the quality of the save was exaggerated in media reports. Full-back Tommy Gemmell had to deputise in goal, and the closing minutes saw Celtic defend desperately. Had extra time been forced, Ayr United would have stood an outstanding chance of capitalising on Celtic's goalkeeping plight rather than going down in history as gallant losers.

Ayr United: Stewart. Malone, Murphy, Fleming, Quinn, Mitchell, Young, Ferguson, Ingram, McCulloch and Rough. *Substitute:* Hood.

Celtic: Fallon, Hay, Gemmell, Dalglish, McNeill, Clark, Hood, Lennox, Wallace, Callaghan and Hughes. *Substitute:* Auld.

After a dramatic six-goal thriller, this programme was hastily compiled for the replay.

AIRDRIE v. AYR UNITED

9 October 1971
Broomfield Park

Scottish League First Division

This game was memorable for a great individual scoring feat and an equally outstanding comeback. It was the old story about victory being snatched from the jaws of defeat. With half an hour of this game left, victory was an awesome task even for a team fired up by Ally MacLeod's optimism.

At the time of this match, Airdrie had been going through a phase of leaking large numbers of goals. They had contrived to lose their three previous League games by a 5-0 scoreline each time. After nine minutes of this match, further misery was visited upon a defence which was experiencing a torrid time on a weekly basis. A move involving Alex Ingram and Joe Filippi culminated in Johnny Graham driving the ball behind Gourlay in the Airdrie goal. Five minutes later, John Whiteford (whose father had signed for Ayr United in 1939) took a free-kick, which was headed home by his cousin, Derek Whiteford. This arrested the scoring drought which had stricken Airdrie. Having rediscovered the art of scoring, the home team let the momentum roll, although the next goal did not come until the fourth minute of the second half, after Davie Stewart had been penalised for handling outside the box. Tommy Walker sent the resultant free-kick into the back of the Ayr net.

With sixty minutes on the clock, Tommy Walker again sent a dead ball into the Ayr net; this time it was from a penalty kick awarded against Ian Campbell for bringing Derek Whiteford down. Airdrie 3 Ayr United 1 – was there any conceivable hope? The situation was even more depressing when weighed against the club's away form … or lack of it. To this point of the season, five away games had been played (League Cup 3; League 2). Four of these games had been lost, although it was of considerable consolation that the solitary win was at Kilmarnock. The previous season, just two away League wins had been recorded in the entire First Division campaign. These wins had been over Cowdenbeath and St Mirren, the two clubs who went down. To put it more succinctly, statistical analysis did not indicate an Ayr United comeback.

Yet some reserves of energy were found, with the result that the two-goal deficit had only to be endured for five minutes. A move involving George McLean and John Doyle culminated in the latter passing to Johnny Graham, who rounded the goalkeeper to lodge the ball in the net. When John Doyle was downed in the penalty area, a gilt-edged chance to level the match was presented. Johnny Graham netted the spot-kick for an equaliser. Thirteen minutes now remained. Was it too optimistic to harbour ambitions of completing the comeback with a winning goal? The momentum continued to roll. In the eighty-third minute, that man Graham neatly controlled a Davie McCulloch cross and then scored with a low shot from about ten yards. From 3-1 down to 4-3 up! The travelling fans were ecstatic.

While many were filtering towards the exits, Alex Ingram put the ball in the Airdrie net once more. It was disallowed for a palpable offside decision. There was not even the remotest possibility that the goal would stand and the supporters knew it, but the mood was so light that a mock celebration took place anyway.

This was Ayr United's last League win until Christmas Day. It was difficult to comprehend why such a spectacular comeback should have preceded such a disappointing run of results.

More positively, it is befitting to single out Johnny Graham's feat in scoring all four goals. It was a feat which he repeated later in the season, when Partick Thistle visited on 29 April

---

Airdrie 3
D. Whiteford, Walker (2)

Ayr United 4
Graham (4)

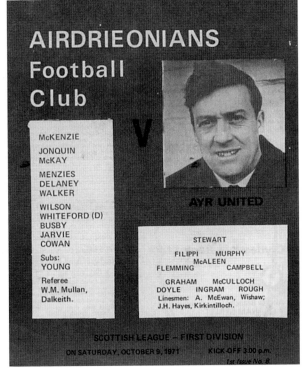

Programme cover.

Johnny Graham sports the penguin-style shirt, two years after his four-goal burst at Airdrie.

1972 and were beaten 4-0. However, the 1971/72 season included three matches in which four goals were netted by an Ayr United player. George McLean also achieved the feat in the course of a 4-2 home win against Dundee United on 15 April 1972.

Airdrie: Gourlay, Jonquin, McKay, Menzies, Delaney, Walker, J. Whiteford, D. Whiteford, Busby, Jarvie and Wilson. *Substitute:* Cowan.

Ayr United: Stewart, Filippi, Murphy, Fleming, Quinn, Campbell, Doyle, Graham, Ingram, McCulloch and Rough. *Substitute:* McLean.

Ayr United v. Rangers

2 September 1972
Somerset Park

Scottish League First Division

In the four seasons from 1969/70 until 1972/73 inclusive, Rangers lost all except one of the League matches which they played at Ayr. It meant that this particular win was far from unexpected. In fact, it was so routine that it was borderline for inclusion in this book. The swaying factor was that Ayr United were part-time, whilst Rangers were the holders of the European Cup Winners Cup. Another important factor about this fixture was that it was a grudge match. Despite the date, it was the third meeting between the clubs so far in the 1972/73 season. The other meetings had been in a League Cup section and Ayr United had lost 2-1 each time. In particular, the Ibrox defeat had rankled because even the Rangers players and fans had expressed amazement that the decisive goal had stood. Davie Stewart, in the Ayr goal, had been wrestled to the ground before being dispossessed. The return tie was played at Rugby Park, due to an incomplete returfing operation at Somerset Park. That was in the midweek prior to this re-match in the opening League fixture; it coincided with the reopening of the ground.

The loss of a fourth-minute goal may have given rise to an impression that Rangers were going to get their way again. Ally McLean in the Ayr goal was beaten by a low drive from Willie Johnston. Once four more minutes had elapsed, it was 1-1. Eric Stevenson cut the ball back for John Doyle to strike a shot which evaded the grasp of Peter McCloy. It is a little-known fact that Peter McCloy had an uncle who had been an Ayr United goalkeeper. The player's name was Henry McCloy, but he only made one competitive appearance (in August 1937).

The early goalscoring flurry may have indicated that a high-scoring match was going to unfold. In reality, there was only one more goal to come. It was scored by a vintage Alex Ingram header; the type of goal that Dixie was renowned for. The scoring action may have subsided after thirty-six minutes, but the rest of the match was certainly not blighted with inaction. Composure was shown throughout, and even the loss of Johnny Graham through injury failed to upset the fluency. He was replaced by Davie McCulloch, who was also able to demonstrate midfield creativity. Rangers should have posed an attacking threat through Willie Johnston and Colin Stein. Perhaps they would have, had it not been for the iron resolve of Alex McAnespie and Stan Quinn. Tommy McLean was marked out of the game by the close attention of John Murphy, and John Doyle was at his incisive best, while Alex Ingram gave the Rangers defence a hard time with his predatory instinct.

There was a temporary scare in the closing minutes when desperation had crept into the Rangers team. The source of the scare was an effort from Jim Denny. Ally McLean had to make a fantastic save to ensure that the points were staying at Ayr. When considered in the light of Ally MacLeod's selection difficulties, the result was even more satisfactory. Injury had ruled out Davie Stewart, Dougie Mitchell, George McLean and Bobby Rough. Essential to the victory was the manner in which the Ayr players refused to be drawn into the type of physical battle which Rangers teams of this era thrived on. It was a victory for skill and composure.

Ayr United 2
Doyle, Ingram

Rangers 1
Johnston

SOMERSET NEWS 5p

SCOTTISH FIRST DIVISION

72 **AYR UNITED** 73

versus

RANGERS

Somerset Park, Ayr

Saturday, 2nd September

Kick-off 1500 hrs.

Programme cover.

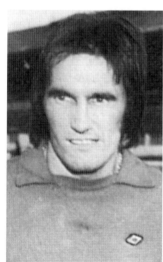

Ally McLean.

Ayr United: McLean, Filippi, Murphy, McAnespie, Quinn, Fleming, Doyle, Graham, Ingram, McGovern and Stevenson. *Substitute:* McCulloch.

Rangers: McCloy, Jardine, Mathieson, Greig, Jackson, Johnstone, McLean, Denny, Johnston, Stein and Fyfe. *Substitute:* MacDonald.

Partick Thistle v. Ayr United

17 March 1973
Firhill Park

Scottish Cup Quarter-Final
Attendance: 10,939

Ayr United's Scottish Cup run began inauspiciously in 1973. Inverness Thistle were dispatched 3-0 at Somerset Park prior to a further home draw against Stirling Albion. The Stirling tie was won 2-1 and it was far from clearcut. In the final minute, Davie Wells headed the ball against the underside of his own crossbar. At least, that was the Ayr version. According to the Stirling version, he headed the ball against the roof of the net. It was indeed fortunate that referee Tommy Marshall did not feel inclined to award a goal.

This took the club through to the quarter-final stage and, although not being favoured with a further home draw, the pairings were relatively kind. Partick Thistle away was considered winnable. Ayr United had, after all, already taken full points from the two League meetings between the clubs that season.

Up until now, no Ayr United team had reached a Scottish Cup semi-final. The club had been robbed of a last four place in 1924 and the quarter-finals of 1938, 1951, 1960 and 1964 had also proven to be unsuccessful. Here, in 1973, the club was enjoying its best season in living memory, but it still seemed a fanciful notion to reach a stage which had never before been achieved. Yet, in practical terms, it was all down to beating a team which Ayr United had already proven they could beat.

Both sets of fans were in great voice. Unfortunately, it was still an age when segregation arrangements were primitive, and emotions spilled over early on in the tie. Crowd disorder was actually in progress when Partick Thistle took the lead. The goal came from a Frank Coulston shot, which entered the net via a post. The positive aspect was that just ten minutes had been played.

There was a magnificent response to the setback. Fifteen minutes after going behind, Davie Wells struck a free-kick which entered the Partick Thistle goalmouth, only to be returned. The clearance fell kindly for Davie McCulloch, who drove the ball high past Alan Rough.

Davie Wells was a key player in the continued fightback. He had earned considerable repute as an overlapping full-back. In the month before this tie, he had been an unused substitute for a Scotland v. England Under-23 international at Rugby Park. Nevertheless, his inclusion in the squad demonstrated at least some recognition, and it is worth mentioning that team-mate John Doyle actually played in the match. When Doyle released Davie Wells, he proceeded to beat three opponents and then cross a low ball, which Davie McCulloch managed to head into the Thistle net. Just two minutes remained until half-time, thereby rendering it a convenient time to take the lead.

Ally MacLeod was not content to allow his team to sit deep and defend the slender lead. In the sixty-third minute, a Johnny Graham cross fell for George McLean to slide home. It was now possible to harbour the notion of the club making history, and the fans knew it. The mood was one of high excitement. In the eighty-first minute, Campbell, the Partick Thistle centre-half, blatantly punched clear an Alex McAnespie free-kick, which inevitably led to a penalty-kick. The responsibility for taking it was entrusted to George McLean. A goal stood to ensure that any lingering doubts would be banished. Alan Rough was a top-class goal-keeper, but this was a day when things were falling into place for Ayr United. McLean scored to create yet more delirium on the terraces – at 4-1, it was known that the tie was won.

In the closing minutes, the injured Davie McCulloch had to be taken off. On his way off, Ally MacLeod was waiting to give him a deserved hug. Even at this stage, the scoring was

---

Partick Thistle 1
Coulston

Ayr United 5
McCulloch (2), McLean (2)
Doyle

Above: Davie McCulloch.

Right: Programme cover.

incomplete. In the final minute, a ball from Davie Wells landed nicely for John Doyle, who cut infield before driving home a further goal. Shortly afterwards, time was called on an ever-to-be-remembered 5-1 triumph.

In January 1877, Ayr Thistle had contested a Scottish Cup semi-final in which a 9-0 defeat had been suffered against Vale of Leven. This was the only semblance of local precedent. Ayr Thistle are one of the clubs in the Ayr United family tree. However, the semi-final of 1973 bore no resemblance to that of 1877 as the margin of defeat was 2-0. The tie in question was a Hampden date against Rangers, and it is remembered mainly for Alex Ingram's disallowed goal in the first minute.

Partick Thistle: Rough, Hansen, Gray, Glavin, Campbell, Strachan, Gibson, Coulston, McQuade, Rae and Lawrie. *Substitute:* Chalmers.

Ayr United: Stewart, Wells, Murphy, McAnespie, Fleming, Filippi, Doyle, Graham, Ingram, McLean and McCulloch. *Substitute:* Campbell.

STRANRAER v. AYR UNITED

16 February 1974   Scottish Cup Fourth Round
Stair Park

The third round Scottish Cup draw was kind to Ayr United in 1974. It can be a mistake to take too much for granted in football, but the assumption was that Cowdenbeath would be swept away, even on their own Central Park. A scoreline of Cowdenbeath 0 Ayr United 5 did not create a blaze of publicity. There was a little sensation of novelty at this being the club's first ever competitive match on a Sunday. Hitherto, no one could have claimed to have seen Ayr United play on a Sunday unless that individual had travelled to Norway in 1928. After eliminating Cowdenbeath, the fourth round draw was awaited with eager anticipation. The anticipation was satisfied with the news that either Stranraer or St Mirren would be played away from home. These clubs had drawn 1-1 at Stranraer and Paisley respectively.

It emerged as a bonus when the second replay was scheduled for Somerset Park on the first Monday in February. In a 3-2 win for Stranraer, the winning goal was a penalty kick from former Ayr United player Ronnie McColl. The prospect of having to go to Stair Park was then viewed in a similar manner to the Cowdenbeath trip in the previous round. Traditionally, matches between Ayr United and Stranraer are referred to as derbies, despite the towns being separated by more than fifty miles. Yet, whether or not this tie could be defined as a derby, the fans travelled down the A77 in considerable numbers.

The Stranraer manager was Eric Caldow, a former Scotland captain and Rangers legend. In the build-up, he played down his team's chances. Whether he was being a realist or whether he was using psychology can only be guessed at. What is certain is that he would have been relieved that John Doyle was unavailable due to suspension. Alex McAnespie returned after suspension, although the Stranraer attack were to ensure that he had a quiet afternoon's work.

The scoring action began after just eight minutes. Bert Ferguson took a corner-kick which was headed across goal by Alex Ferguson to give Davie McCulloch an easy chance, which he took gratefully. Nine minutes later, another Bert Ferguson corner-kick culminated in a further goal from McCulloch. This time, he struck with a header after goalkeeper Gallacher had touched the ball in his direction. At 2-0, the steam was taken out of the tie and half-time arrived with no further scoring having taken place.

In a devastating eighteen-minute spell in the second half, five goals were scored. The scoring momentum began in the sixty-first minute and, yet again, a corner-kick was the source. It was taken short to Alex Ferguson, who cut the ball back to Johnny Graham. Graham, the club captain, proceeded to score with a shot that was deflected into the net via the head of Stranraer full-back McAuley. Several minutes later, George McLean made it 4-0 with a shot which definitely did not take a deflection. He took a pass from Johnny Graham to viciously lash the ball into the net from an angle. Bert Ferguson was then downed by McCutcheon for a penalty kick. By this means, Davie McCulloch got his hat-trick. Even at 5-0, the scoring action persisted. A long clearance from Alex McAnespie put George McLean in the clear and he found the net with a neatly placed shot. A further visit to that end saw Gallacher save brilliantly from a Graham drive. Somewhat harshly, he was unable to recover the loose ball and George McLean fired it in to complete the second hat-trick of the tie.

At 7-0 up with eleven minutes left, there was a visible slackening-off. In the eighty-third minute, Hugh Hay scored for Stranraer with a header. The cross had been supplied by Denis Gray – one of three former Ayr United players in the home team. The others were Ronnie McColl and Jim Flynn.

Stranraer 1
Hay

Ayr United 7
McCulloch (3), Graham,
McLean (3)

STRANRAER FOOTBALL CLUB

versus

AYR UNITED

SCOTTISH CUP — FOURTH ROUND

SAT., 16th FEBRUARY, 1974

Kick-off 3 p.m.

Official Programme

2p

Stranraer v. Ayr United

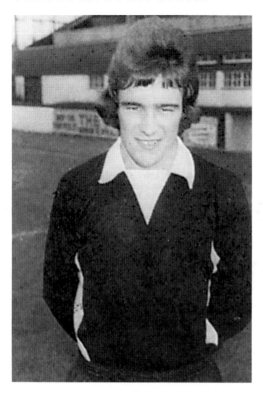

Bert Ferguson.

Prior to this tie, the last time an Ayr United player had scored a hat-trick in the Scottish Cup was when Peter Price did so against Airdrie in February 1960. It was therefore an excellent achievement for Davie McCulloch *and* George McLean to do it in the same tie. After 1974, the next Scottish Cup hat-trick by an Ayr United player was scored by Ian Ferguson against Alloa in January 1998.

Despite wearing the striker's number nine shirt, Alex Ferguson did not get onto the score-sheet at Stranraer, but he could reflect on being involved in setting up some of the goals. Of the spectators who attended, no one could have predicted that one of the players on view would go on to gain a knighthood for services to football.

In competitive matches, no Ayr United team had ever won away from home with a margin exceeding six goals. A club record would therefore have been created in the event of avoiding the loss of a late goal. In the event, it comprised a shared record. In January 2002, another gilt-edged chance to create a new record was missed. When 6-0 up against Deveronvale, a penalty was saved and the score remained unchanged.

What happened after the rout of Stranraer? A 1-1 draw was achieved against Hearts in a quarter-final tie, with a Tynecastle Park attendance of 17,219. The replay was lost 2-1 after extra time in front of a crowd of 16,185. Yet Ayr United managed to take full League points against Hearts in 1973/74.

Stranraer: Gallacher, Hopkins, McAuley, McCutcheon, Heap, Hay, McColl, Gray, Flynn, Traynor and Campbell. *Substitutes:* Malone and Bark.

Ayr United: A. McLean, Filippi, Murphy, McAnespie, Fleming, Mitchell, R. Ferguson, Graham, A. Ferguson, G. McLean and McCulloch. *Substitutes:* Bell and Ingram.

11 October 1975   Premier Division
Somerset Park

The 1975/76 season saw a radical change to the structure of Scottish football when the two-league set-up was increased to three leagues. By virtue of the position gained in the old-style First Division of 1974/75, Ayr United were included in the first batch of clubs to play in the new upper echelon. There were snipers who indicated that the club would not survive the ultra-competitive nature of the new set-up, whose argument was based on the fact that Ayr United continued to have part-time status. Yet sometimes this status was a benefit when it came to luring new players. The opportunity to combine football with a working career afforded security. However, on balance, it should have amounted to a handicap, but there were times when opposing teams could be not only matched, but outmatched, for commitment and fitness.

1975/76 was a season in which Rangers were destined to win the League, the Scottish Cup and the Scottish League Cup. This is mentioned in order to put some kind of perspective on what happened at Somerset Park on an autumn afternoon in 1975. Putting it further into perspective is the fact that it was necessary to play the bulk of this match with a limping goalkeeper, since Hugh Sproat hurt himself in an early clash with striker Derek Parlane. At this point in history, it was possible to name two substitutes and it was extremely rare for a manager to list a back-up goalkeeper. Ally MacLeod's substitutes for this match were Jim McSherry and Hugh Cameron – a midfielder and a striker!

It was an afternoon when John Doyle just could not be stopped. He inflicted ninety minutes of torment on a defence which just could not cope with him. The tackling was heavy, but his speed ensured that he was seldom caught up in it. Doyle was the most prominent figure in the opening stages, despite the near loss of a goal. A back-header from Derek Johnstone cleared the Ayr United crossbar by an uncomfortably close margin. On springing back into attack, an Alex Ingram drive was beaten out by Rangers goalkeeper Peter McCloy. Joe Filippi seized onto the rebound and shot wide. In a subsequent attack, John Doyle succeeded in taking the ball round Peter McCloy, only to find the angle too tight for a shot. He therefore elected for the sensible option of cutting it back. Ian McDougall reacted quickest to the cutback and cleared the danger.

The balance of the game indicated that Ayr United looked more like scoring. It proved to be an accurate indication. In the twenty-eighth minute, the vastly experienced John Greig hit a poor passback which was picked up by Gerry Phillips, who killed the ball and neatly set up Davie McCulloch. After rounding McDougall, McCulloch scored with a low shot. It was reasonably expected that this would sting Rangers into attack. In the immediate aftermath of Davie McCulloch's goal, the luxury of chasing an equaliser was not afforded to Rangers. Ayr United pressed into attack once more, and that man Doyle struck a shot which Peter McCloy failed to hold. The ball fell to Alex Ingram, who easily made it 2-0. This goal came within a minute of the re-centre. For the remainder of the first half, the two-goal lead was not threatened. Then, when the teams re-emerged, it was obvious that the Rangers players had been subject to some choice words by their manager, Jock Wallace. Alex McAnespie had to clear a Derek Johnstone header off the line, and then Hugh Sproat did well to touch an Ian McDougall drive over the crossbar. When Colin Jackson was booked for pulling at Gerry Phillip's shirt, this was a clear indication that Rangers were rattled. Thirteen minutes into the second half, they were rattled still further. Davie McCulloch released John Doyle, who beat

Ayr United 3   Rangers 0
McCulloch, Ingram, Graham

Ayr United v. Rangers

The Ayr United defence coped with everything that came their way on 11 October 1975. The Ayr players shown are, from left to right, Hugh Sproat, Davie Wells, Joe Filippi and the partly hidden Rikki Fleming.

Alex Miller with ease and then sent over a cross which Johnny Graham drove home, despite the close attention of John Greig.

At 3-0, the white-shirted players still did not seem content. Peter McCloy did well to stop a Doyle drive, whilst another attack concluded with Alex Ingram slamming a shot against a post.

As the game drew towards a conclusion, there were a couple of talking points. Alex Miller was extremely lucky to escape punishment for an assault on John Doyle. This preceded an incident in which Doyle, while in the vicinity of the touchline on the far side, showed off his crucifix to the Rangers supporters near the front of the terracing. It was an action which triggered a predictably angry response. Was he motivated by the earlier incident with Alex Miller?

Having beaten Rangers with an ease which, at times, was contemptuous, Alex Ingram later commented: 'Why should a Premier League team like ourselves be over the moon at beating Rangers?', proving that the contempt did not end at the final whistle.

Ayr United: Sproat, Wells, Murphy, McAnespie, Fleming, Filippi, Doyle, Graham, Ingram, Phillips and McCulloch. *Substitutes:* McSherry and Cameron.

Rangers: McCloy, Jardine, Dawson, Greig, Jackson, McDonald, McLean, McDougall, Parlane, Johnstone and Scott. *Substitutes:* Miller and McKean.

SOMERSET NEWS

VOL. 6
No. 6

10p

SCOTTISH PREMIER LEAGUE

AYR UNITED

versus

RANGERS

SATURDAY, 11th OCTOBER

Kick-off 1500 hrs.

Ayr United v. Motherwell

3 May 1976
Somerset Park

Premier Division

On Saturday, 6 March 1976, an Ayr United v. Celtic game was postponed because Celtic claimed difficulty in being able to field a strong enough team. Their fear of playing at Ayr stemmed from the fact that five of their players were suffering from 'flu. The game was rescheduled for Wednesday 10 March. Again it was postponed on the grounds that Celtic felt unable to field a strong enough team. On 13 March, Motherwell should have played at Ayr. The game did not proceed on that date because Motherwell also claimed that they had players suffering from 'flu. As a result, these matches were tagged on to the end of the season, which meant that Ayr United faced a run-in which comprised Celtic (away), Celtic (home) and Motherwell (home).

Despite a result reading Celtic 1 Ayr United 2, the last two matches had still to be faced with the haunting fear of relegation hanging over them. One week later, Celtic were trailing 3-1 at Somerset Park with half an hour to go. The eventual consequences of losing 5-3 were potentially severe. With Motherwell due at Ayr on the Monday, the position was frightening.

St Johnstone were long since doomed to relegation. In order for Ayr United not to join them, it was necessary to obtain a draw against Motherwell and hope that Rangers would beat Dundee United the next night. Taking the view that the Dundee United score could not be relied upon, a win was necessary. It transpired that Rangers v. Dundee United was a goalless draw on the Tuesday. The Motherwell manager at this time was Willie McLean whose brother Jim, the Dundee United manager, would have been relieved of the need to draw at Ibrox in the event of a Motherwell win at Ayr. The other club in the equation was Dundee. They stood to be relegated in the event of an Ayr win and a Dundee United draw. In retrospect, it may seem complicated but, at the start of May 1976, all connected to Ayr United knew the situation with total clarity. It was not even necessary to unravel the scenarios in order to understand the aim which was: beat Motherwell, or else!

Alex Stuart had injury problems to contemplate. This necessitated the young and inexperienced John Hyslop being given a place in the starting line-up. Despite the tension of the occasion, he proceeded to have an excellent match.

Stewart Rennie went on to render Ayr United fine service later in his career but, at this time, he was the Motherwell goalkeeper. Early in the match, he was tested twice by headers from Gerry Phillips. This was indicative of a promising start. Alas, the promise was not fulfilled. With ten minutes played, Pat Gardner struck a drive which beat Hugh Sproat, who may have been unsighted in the busy penalty area. In 1969, Gardner had scored for Dunfermline Athletic against West Bromwich Albion to put his club into the semi-final of the European Cup Winners Cup, therefore it is unlikely that this goal at Ayr would have been a career highlight, especially since this was his last match for Motherwell prior to a summer move to Arbroath. Yet, from an Ayr United perspective, the goal carried potentially severe repercussions.

Much effort was expended in an attempt to correct what had turned into a bleak scenario. Up front, Gerry Phillips worked hard in pursuit of an opening, although Alex Ingram came closest to obtaining an equaliser during the rest of the first half. From close range, he sent a header too high. The half-time whistle was not a welcome sound.

In the 1970s, a feature of matches against Motherwell was Alex Ingram's personal rivalry with opposing centre-half Willie McVie. They were both hard men, and the fans used to be

---

Ayr United 2
McCulloch, Phillips

Motherwell 1
Gardner

Premier League football was maintained for 1976/77, the season in which this photograph was taken.

enthralled at the prospect of who would come off best when they met. With sixty-two minutes played, McVie fouled his adversary at the cost of a penalty kick. Amidst mounting tension, the ball was placed on the spot at the Railway End. Then came the moment of decision. Stewart Rennie dived in the opposite direction to Malcolm Robertson's kick. However, the ball went wide. This was worrying and frustrating in equal measure. Yet, in analysing this match, it would be wrong to be critical of Robertson. Had it not been for his late season form, Ayr United would have been doomed to relegation before now.

Rather than wilt, the match was still gamely pursued. This perseverance paid off with fifteen minutes left. A cross from Jim McSherry was dropped by Rennie to afford Davie McCulloch the grateful opportunity to poke the ball over the line. Time might have been played out on a 1-1 draw, had it been fatally assumed that Rangers were going to beat Dundee United on the next night. The wisdom of taking the view that only victory would suffice eventually pushed the players towards survival. Five minutes after drawing level, the ball was on its way out for what would have been a corner-kick to Ayr United. Davie McCulloch did not give up on it and managed to get in a cross, which Gerry Phillips scrambled into the net. Nobody cared that it could not have been defined as a classic strike. All around the ground, the fans were going berserk. However, within seconds, they were going berserk for a totally different reason. Referee Alistair McKenzie signalled a corner-kick in the belief that the ball had already crossed the by-line before the cutback. This was a crushing disappointment. Some hope then emerged. Whether in response to the protests or of his own volition, the referee went over to consult a linesman. During their discussion, the crowd experienced a tension which bordered on terror. Mr McKenzie then turned and indicated a goal. This time the fans staged celebrations which were not so abruptly curtailed.

Ayr United v. Motherwell

League Goals 1975/76	
Graham	16
Doyle	6
Robertson	6
Ingram	5
McCulloch	4
Phillips	4
Wells	2
Fleming	1
McDonald	1
Murphy	1
Total	**46**

Gerry Phillips.

Could the 2-1 lead be defended for the final ten minutes? In theory, there was only pride at stake for Motherwell, yet throughout this match they displayed a level of commitment that could have given the impression that they were one of the clubs in peril. Davie McCulloch got himself booked for time-wasting. His motivation for this misdemeanour was understandable. What happened next was neatly described in the *Glasgow Herald*.

'When the referee blew for full time, the fans spilled onto the pitch and the players had to run a gauntlet of hands that reached out to slap backs and ruffle sweat-streaked hair. The overjoyed supporters refused to leave the pitch until their heroes had taken a bow. The fans chanted, sang, and even wept as the players appeared in the stand to wave to them. Then John Murphy, the captain, and his men applauded the fans. It was emotional ... the kind of scene that makes football the great game it is.'

Ayr United: Sproat, Filippi, Murphy, Fleming, Tait, Hyslop, Phillips, McSherry, Ingram, McCulloch and Robertson. *Substitutes:* McDonald and Kelly.
Motherwell: Rennie, McLaren, Wark, Watson, McVie, Stevens, Marinello, Gardner, Graham, Davidson and McAdam. *Substitutes:* Millar and Kennedy.

In the 1987/88 season, a club record points total was achieved. A haul of sixty-one points was one better than the previous best, which had been achieved in 1958/59. Of course, this was in an age when it was still on the basis of two points for a win. Three points for a win was introduced in Scotland at the outset of 1994/95. The club record on that basis was the total of seventy-seven, which was reached in 1996/97. Points may have propelled Ayr United to the Second Division title in 1987/88, but the issue of goals was much more exciting. This was the Sludden/Templeton era, and the goals just kept on flowing. It was a euphoric time, when Saturdays just could not come along quickly enough.

On 12 September 1987, Ayr United won 6-1 at Cowdenbeath. Not since 14 October 1978 had the club last managed six goals in a League fixture (Montrose 4 Ayr United 6). What had taken almost nine years to achieve, was to take only three more weeks to repeat.

The Stenhousemuir programme for the Ayr match contained some clinical editorial. Readers were told that: 'After Monday night's board meeting, the board of Stenhousemuir Football Club unanimously decided to dismiss the manager, William Henderson, and his coaching staff. The board felt that the results of late and general performance of the team were not of the standard they had hoped for and they felt it was time for a change. Stenhousemuir Football Club would like to thank Alex Rennie for stepping in as caretaker at such short notice.'

For Alex Rennie, it was to be the proverbial baptism of fire. After sixteen minutes, a pass from Ian McAllister was controlled by John Sludden, who then chipped the ball over home goalkeeper Stuart Robertson. The goal was both clinical and efficient. A precise crowd figure was not issued for this game; even enquiries directly to Ochilview Park brought forth nothing more than an estimated figure. Newspapers reported wildly conflicting figures. The actual attendance looked to be in the region of 1,800, the vast majority of whom had decanted east in support of Ayr United. These fans were not there in the hope of seeing a modest 1-0 win. It was known that the firepower was there to pull off a rout. As the first half wound on, it was therefore mildly disappointing that Ayr United's superiority did not manifest itself in more scoring until seven minutes before the break. It was a goal which might have been scored by Sludden but, to his credit, he squared the ball to the better-placed Jim Cowell, who had little difficulty in shooting past Robertson.

In the minutes leading up to half-time, Stenhousemuir had their best spell of the match. In rapid succession, they won three corner-kicks. Tom Condie would have had a simple chance to put the ball into an empty Ayr net but, thankfully, he failed to connect. In contrast, his team-mate David Beaton connected powerfully when taking a free-kick. It took a fantastic save from George Watson to keep the goal intact.

From the start of the second half, Stenhousemuir were finished as an attacking force. Fans delayed overlong in the half-time pie queues were to miss the third goal. Stevie McIntyre and Tommy Walker were instrumental in initiating a move in which possession came the way of John Sludden. Possession switched from Sludden to Templeton and back to Sludden, who had the poise to chest the ball down before slamming it into the net. Sludden was now chasing a hat-trick, and he went so close to clinching it when shooting against the crossbar.

In the sixty-sixth minute, Ayr United scored a goal of breathtaking quality. After taking a pass from Sludden, Jim Cowell drove the ball into the top corner of the net from the edge of

---

Stenhousemuir 0

Ayr United 6
*Sludden (2), Cowell (2), Walker,
Templeton*

STENHOUSEMUIR v. AYR UNITED

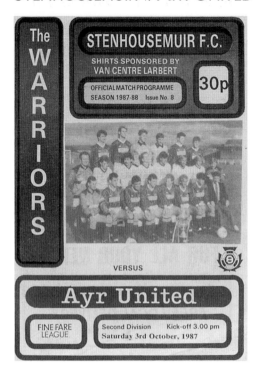

Official match programme cover.

the penalty area. Amidst mounting glee, the score was taken to 5-0 two minutes later. The initial shot was from Henry Templeton, but the ball was diverted past Robertson by Tommy Walker, to whom the goal was credited.

In what remained of the game, the home players were visibly dispirited. A beleaguered Stenhousemuir defender even slammed a full-blooded drive against his own post in the closing minutes. It was unclear what he was trying to do. However, the incident did create some mirth amongst the fans situated behind that goal. The only issues to be resolved were the scale of the victory and the question of whether John Sludden would get his fourth hat-trick of the season. In pursuit of this quest, he had a near miss with a shot. A subsequent attempt was stopped on the line by the hand of full-back Harry Cairney. It was a blatant penalty-kick award, but Sludden must have felt frustrated at being denied in such a manner. He did not even get the opportunity to score from the spot. That job was satisfactorily completed by Henry Templeton. Four minutes later, time was called. It is often the case that fans will depart from a one-sided game with the opinion that 'it could have been ten'. In reality, it could have been. The top of the Second Division then looked like this.

	P	W	D	L	F	A	Pts
Ayr United	10	8	2	0	33	5	18

Ally MacLeod did have one concern. He expressed concern about the fans encroaching on the pitch during goal celebrations. It was a valid point, yet it was symptomatic of progress that the exuberance had reached such a scale. These were happy days.

Stenhousemuir: Robertson, Cairney, Gillen, Walker, Beaton, Erwin, Quinn, McCafferty, Condie, Thomson, Jamieson. *Substitutes:* McIntosh and Buchanan.

Ayr United: Watson, McIntyre, Hughes, Furphy, McAllister, Evans, Templeton, Scott, Walker, Sludden and Cowell. *Substitutes:* Wilson and McCracken.

KILMARNOCK v. AYR UNITED

13 August 1996   Coca-Cola Cup Second Round
Rugby Park   Attendance: 8,543

At the start of the 1996/97 season, Ayr United could not reflect on a good recent history in the League Cup. Not since 1991 had the club managed to score in the competition. In 1996, the first round draw entailed a home match with Livingston and, at the time of that tie, it was already known that the winners would face Kilmarnock at Rugby Park. It was an excellent incentive to break the scoring drought. The challenge of Livingston was easily brushed aside with a 5-2 scoreline that did not even convey the true extent of Ayr United's dominance.

At this time, Ayr United had Second Division status, whilst Kilmarnock were well established in the Premier League. They were also destined to win that season's Scottish Cup. The prospect of going there should have been daunting, but it wasn't. Whether born out of naivety or blind faith, the tie was approached with sufficient bravado as to instil a belief that it was winnable. The ensuing seasons would see a series of cup meetings between the Ayrshire rivals; more than one of which would be approached with trepidation. In theory, this tie in 1996 should have been approached with greater trepidation than these future ties, but that was not the mood of the chirpy fans who descended on Rugby Park on that summer night.

A key player in this tie was Robert Connor. Ayr United had sold him to Dundee in the summer of 1984, and further moves took him to Dundee, Aberdeen and Kilmarnock. He was released by Kilmarnock in the summer of 1996, and his next move brought him full-circle to Ayr United. The Coca-Cola Cup therefore afforded him the opportunity of an unexpectedly quick return to Rugby Park. Connor did not score at all for Kilmarnock during his two seasons there; hence the irony of what was about to happen.

Twelve minutes into the tie, Steve Kerrigan attempted a diving header in response to an Isaac English cross. The ball then came off Killie defender Neil Whitworth and landed for Robert Connor to score in clinical fashion. With most of the Ayr support housed behind the goal at the Rugby Road end, this goal was seen from a good vantage point. The general mood in that stand was one of delirium.

After tangling with future Ayr United player Derek Anderson, Steve Kerrigan was yellow-carded for his involvement. In addition to this, he suffered a badly injured left hand in the same incident. It had to be bandaged. Kerrigan was the first of five Ayr United players to be booked, the referee's book gradually filling up with the names of Bobby Law, Darren Henderson, Gregg Hood and Robert Connor. It was a source of concern that so many players were just one misdemeanour away from being dismissed, particularly in view of the competitive nature of the tie. Kilmarnock, with only Paul Wright booked, were not similarly burdened.

Throughout the match, Killie manager Alex Totten was excessively animated. He gesticulated frantically and shouted vociferously in an attempt to push his team to greater efforts. At half-time, with his team still a goal in arrears, the message would have been plain. When the second half got underway, Kilmarnock did push forward with a renewed sense of urgency. Yet the main task of Henry Smith, aged forty at this time, was to pick routine crosses out of the air. However, Ayr United were not impotent in attack. In the sixty-second minute, the fans were on their feet to acclaim a second goal from a point-blank header by Gregg Hood. The acclaim was premature. Goalkeeper Lekovic clawed the ball back and play continued. With the bulk of the Ayr support situated at the opposite end of the ground, it was put down to a near thing when viewed from afar. In the aftermath of the tie, Kilmarnock supporters, with a close vantage point, were honest in their admissions that the ball had crossed the line without doubt.

Kilmarnock 0   **Ayr United 1**
                                      Connor

KILMARNOCK v. AYR UNITED

Darren Henderson makes a crossfield run.

At last, Henry Smith was beaten. With a Jim McIntyre effort dropping towards the net, he was stranded. Bobby Law was situated on the line, but it appeared that the ball was simply going to drop in over his head. Perhaps by gut determination, Law managed to put enough effort into his jump to effect a headed clearance. The Ayr fans roared their approval.

Kilmarnock's attacking threat continued to be of an aerial nature. In the heart of the defence, Gregg Hood, Willie Jamieson and Ronnie Coyle coped admirably. In a desperate, though understandable measure, Lekovic vacated the Kilmarnock goal in order to lend his services to his team's attackers. Alas, his goalkeeping instinct did not desert him and he was fortunate to escape a yellow card for being at the wrong end when he punched the ball.

In the closing minutes, Henry Smith permitted himself the luxury of conducting the loud choir behind him. Gordon Dalziel was not similarly casual in his assumption of victory. He took the precautionary measure of replacing Steve Kerrigan with Paul Kinnaird in order to run the clock down. Then came the final whistle, which was testament to the confidence of Smith.

In the next round, Darren Henderson scored in a 3-1 defeat against Rangers at Ibrox. That goal comprised the club's 500th in the history of the League Cup competition. Yet the milestone goal should have belonged to Gregg Hood for his 'over-the-line' header at Kilmarnock.

Kilmarnock: Lekovic, MacPherson, Tallon, Reilly, Whitworth, Anderson, Mitchell, Henry, Wright, McIntyre and McKee. *Substitutes:* Montgomerie, Roberts and Lauchlan.

Ayr United: H. Smith, Law, Hood, Coyle, Jamieson, Connor, P. Smith, English, Kerrigan, Henderson and George. *Substitutes:* Traynor, Kinnaird and Cameron.

Kilmarnock

FOOTBALL CLUB

Tuesday 13th August 1996   Kick-off 7.30pm

KILMARNOCK V AYR UNITED

COCA-COLA LEAGUE CUP, 2nd ROUND

Season 1996/97 · Issue No 2   Official Match Programme £1.50

BERWICK RANGERS v. AYR UNITED

10 May 1997   Scottish League Second Division
Shielfield Park   Attendance: 1,423

Approaching the concluding week of 1996/97, the top of the Second Division looked like this:

	P	W	D	L	F	A	Pts
Ayr United	35	22	8	5	59	33	74
Hamilton Accies	35	22	7	6	75	28	73

Both clubs were already guaranteed promotion but, since the Accies had a vastly superior goal difference, there was little scope for error in the quest for the championship. In their last match, Hamilton were scheduled to play Livingston at home (Cliftonhill Park, Coatbridge). Ayr United's last match was away against Berwick Rangers. The fans faced a long journey, but the mood was one of excessive optimism since Berwick were rooted to the foot of the table. It would not have been possible to hand-pick better opponents in the circumstances.

The largest League attendance at Shielfield Park to this point of the season had been 564. Their final match drew 1,423 spectators through the turnstiles. A non-segregation policy meant that it was not possible to get a breakdown on the number of Ayr supporters who crossed the border. An estimate of 1,200 would be a reasonably accurate reflection. Ayr United's desire for victory made it a good day for the Berwick Rangers exchequer.

The carnival mood of the fans did not comprise misplaced optimism. Only one League defeat had been suffered out of the last eighteen games played, and even that isolated reverse had included a major injustice which was brought about by a contentious last-minute refereeing decision at Livingston. In the matter of team selection, Gordon Dalziel's only problem was that there were no injury worries and he had to contemplate who to leave out.

When the whistle blew to start the match, Ayr United went straight for the kill. Four corner-kicks were won in the first five minutes. Even this early, it was difficult to envisage the Berwick defence being able to withstand this pressure. The corner-kicks continued to persist. To have kept count would have been a pedantic exercise, but the general pattern correctly indicated the intensive pressure which was applied. Worryingly, chances were being created and missed. *What if* it was going to be one of those frustrating days? *What if* Hamilton Accies were to win? *What if* Berwick Rangers were to hit on the break? To compound the growing unease, Robert Bell, John Traynor and Mark Humphries all hit either the post or crossbar and the game remained scoreless.

Barely two minutes from half-time, Robert Scott broke through and struck a low drive goalward. Home goalkeeper Michael Burgess did well to block the shot. Then the rebound fell to Scott who struck another low drive. This time it evaded the diving goalkeeper and came to rest in the net. Excessive celebrations ensued, albeit that they were partly fuelled by relief.

From the re-centre, possession was quickly regained and another attack launched. Tom Smith found himself in a good shooting position and let loose with an attempt which Burgess pushed away. John Traynor seized on the loose ball near the by-line and cut it back for Alain Horace to fire it home from six yards. Fresh impetus was given to the shouting and singing, and it did not subside when John Rowbotham blew the half-time whistle just a matter of seconds afterwards.

Berwick Rangers 0   **Ayr United 2**
                                               Scott, Horace

Berwick Rangers Football Club

BORDERER'S REVIEW . . .

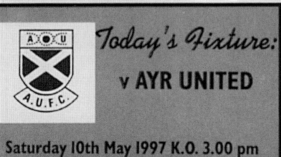

Today's Fixture:

v AYR UNITED

Saturday 10th May 1997 K.O. 3.00 pm
Bells League Division Two
PROGRAMME £1.00

Club Sponsors:

FEDERATION
BREWERY

Kit Sponsors:

AVEC

Match Sponsors:
Harcros
BUILDERS MERCHANTS

Ball Sponsors:
**Ponteland
Auction Mart**

Match Mascot:
Joe Siswick

BELL'S
LEAGUE CHAMPIONSHIP

Berwick Rangers v. Ayr United

Above: Physiotherapist John Kerr is flanked by Steve Kerrigan (with trophy) and Duncan George. Gregg Hood is at the front. *Right:* Darren Henderson admires John Traynor's headgear while Gregg Hood looks on.

The half-time score at the Hamilton Accies *v.* Livingston fixture was 0-0, yet the importance of that result had receded greatly. In the interests of caution, a Hamilton win had to be assumed, but Berwick had shown no threat in the first half. Quite how they had held out until virtually the end of the first half was difficult to comprehend. Ayr United's two-goal cushion was assuredly safe, lest Jimmy Thomson could transform his players dramatically with his half-time pep talk.

The pace was stepped down in the second half as there was no longer a need for attacking abandon. Henry Smith continued to have a quiet afternoon in the Ayr goal, as not even the vaguest resemblance of a threat came his way. Fans with radios conveyed the news that the Hamilton game was still scoreless and was on course to finish that way. As time progressed, the sense of urgency scaled down accordingly, although there were some fleeting moments of excitement. For example, Robert Scott embarked on a solo run from the halfway line, but completed the run by shooting wide.

The stage was reached when the final whistle was yearned for, not that there was any tension in the air. The motive for wishing the game to finish was that the happy fans wished to start celebrating for real. An announcement on the public address system warned that the presentation of the championship trophy would not take place in the event of supporters invading the field. The announcement was effective and captain Ronnie Coyle was duly presented with the silverware, before the field was engulfed.

Berwick Rangers: Burgess, Stewart, Laidler, Finlayson, Reid, Irvine, Ludlow, Little, Clegg, Walton and Graham. *Substitutes:* Grant, Manson and Craig.

Ayr United: H. Smith, Traynor, Humphries, Coyle, Hood, Watson, T. Smith, Horace, Scott, George and Bell. *Substitutes:* Kerrigan, Kinnaird and Henderson.

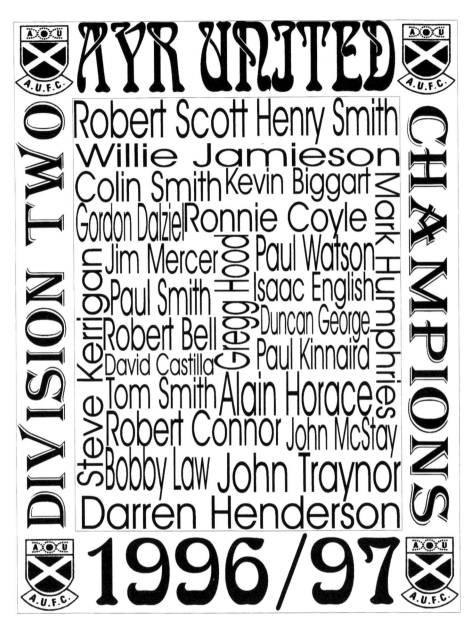

The men who made Ayr United champions.

AYR UNITED v. KILMARNOCK

14 February 1998   Scottish Cup Fourth Round
Somerset Park   Attendance: 9,286

In 1998 the fourth round Scottish Cup draw was not wholly enthused over by the people of Ayr and district. It is true that there was a degree of excitement about the prospect of Somerset Park hosting an Ayrshire derby, but it was an excitement which was tempered by a fear of what might happen. Kilmarnock were the holders of the trophy and this was in contrast to Ayr United's indifferent form in the First Division. In fact, the description 'indifferent' is flattering. A win for Morton on the afternoon of this tie had the effect of landing the club in second bottom place. Neither was history on the side of Ayr United. There was only one previous instance of the club enjoying a home Scottish Cup win against a team from a higher League and that had taken place in 1928. Not that it had been a shock result back then – the club was on course for the Second Division title, whereas opponents Bo'ness were struggling at the foot of the First Division.

Two hours before the scheduled kick-off time, referee Hugh Dallas expressed doubts about whether the tie would proceed. Torrential rain had been falling on the pitch for much of the morning, but there was a reprieve when the groundstaff were permitted an extra half-hour to work on the surface. The go-ahead was given, although the ground was understandably heavy. So bad were the conditions that, before the kick-off, sawdust had to be sprinkled along each goal line in order to replace the whitewash which had disappeared.

The pitch was not conducive to flowing football. It was, however, conducive to hard tackling. The yellow card was shown seven times in this tie and Andy Millen saw it first. His misdemeanour was a foul on Jerome Vareille after fifteen minutes. Team-mate Paul Agnew was the next in the book for a challenge on Gary Holt. Yet Ayr United goalkeeper Kristjan Finnbogason was untroubled by the elements. A typically wet winter's day in Scotland did not remotely constitute a hardship to the Icelandic international. With seventeen minutes played, he blocked a Holt shot which resulted from a Mark Roberts cross. Seven minutes afterwards, a through ball from Gus MacPherson was back-heeled by Vareille into the path of Ally Mitchell, who was thwarted by Finnbogason smothering the ball at his feet.

Kevin McGowne's name joined the others in the book, his crime being a body-check on Gary Bowman. In the thirty-sixth minute, Ayr United took a 3-1 lead in the matter of bookings when Jim Dick uprooted several yards of turf and Gary Holt!

The second half was consistent with the torrid nature of the first half. Of particular concern though, was that Kilmarnock visibly had a strong appetite after the resumption. In the first minute after the restart, Martin Baker went close with a header. Five minutes afterwards, Finnbogason blocked brilliantly from Holt, whilst a subsequent bit of danger was broken up by the on-form Icelander pushing over a Mark Roberts effort from a corner-kick taken by Mitchell. Kilmarnock were showing some incisive qualities at this stage of the tie, but the Ayr defence could not be unlocked. Gradually, it became evident that the tie was far from a lost cause. With sixty-five minutes played, John Traynor steered a header a matter of inches over Gordon Marshall's crossbar. This was just after Laurent Djaffo had come on in place of Keith Hogg. Djaffo was the kind of player who performed better when it was an important occasion. At other times, he was apt to have his attitude questioned. An Ayrshire derby doubling up as a Scottish Cup tie in front of a decent crowd and intensive television coverage; this was just his kind of match.

Ayr United 2   Kilmarnock 0
Dick, Ferguson

98

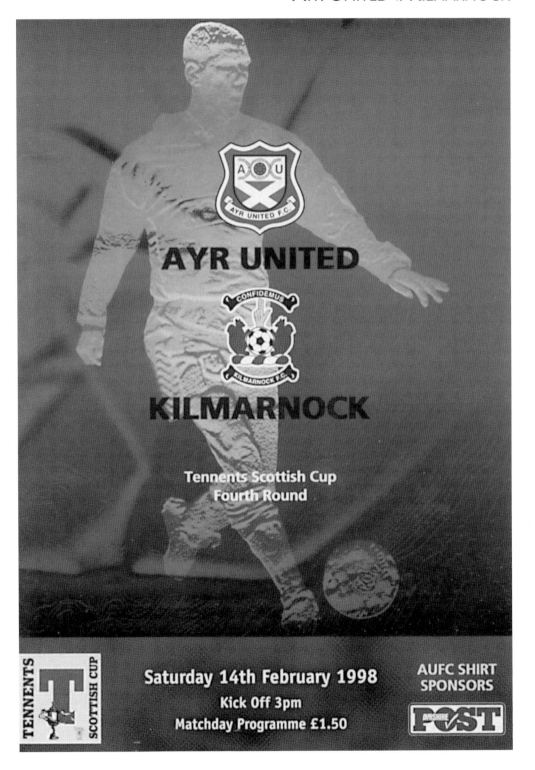

AYR UNITED

KILMARNOCK

Tennents Scottish Cup
Fourth Round

Saturday 14th February 1998
Kick Off 3pm
Matchday Programme £1.50

AUFC SHIRT
SPONSORS

A thirty-yard drive from Holt was brilliantly saved by Kristjan Finnbogason. This was the turning point. In the eighty-third minute, the persistence of Djaffo allowed him to force the ball wide to Ian Ferguson, who crossed it into the Kilmarnock goalmouth. The ball was met at the back post by Jim Dick who headed it into the net. Behind that goal, the fans in the Somerset Road end went wild. On other sides of the ground, this behaviour was replicated in an atmosphere of delirium. Could the final seven minutes now be negotiated safely?

Two minutes later, Djaffo dispossessed the hesitant McGowne, and then cut the ball back to Ian Ferguson, who swivelled before curling a shot into the net at Marshall's left-hand post. The clamour, which had barely died down from the first goal, was now renewed. This time it was not allowed to die down – the fans remained on song right to the end and beyond.

Left: Singing and dancing in the rain. !an Ferguson has made it 2-0.

TENNENTS SCOTTISH CUP FOURTH ROUND

Hogg Djaffo Millen Dick Burns Anderson Traynor Ferguson Agnew Bowman Finnbogason Robertson

2

Dick 83   Ferguson 85

0

9,286

SATURDAY FEBRUARY 14TH 1998

Afterwards, much publicity was accorded to the conditions, implying that they were a contributory factor in the result. In the heat of battle, the turf did cut up, but Ayr United too were prevented from playing silky football. Further publicity was accorded to Kilmarnock doing the greatest share of attacking. The point was stretched to a ridiculous degree, whereby it was suggested that visiting goalkeeper Gordon Marshall did not make a save all afternoon. This was palpable nonsense, although it might be cynically observed that his team's cause would have been better served if he *had* made some more saves.

The next round involved a 4-1 defeat against Hearts, the eventual winners, at Tynecastle Park in the quarter-final. Those who travelled east in such substantial numbers made sure that their vocal chords were well exercised. In the seasons ahead, those same vocal chords stood to be taxed to an even greater degree in the Scottish Cup competition.

Ayr United: Finnbogason, Robertson, Hogg, Millen, Burns, Anderson, Dick, Traynor, Ferguson, Agnew and Bowman. *Substitutes:* Djaffo, Bonar and Castilla.
Kilmarnock: Marshall, MacPherson, Baker, Lauchlan, McGowne, Reilly, Mitchell, Holt, Wright, Roberts and Vareille. *Substitutes:* McIntyre, Bagan and Henry.

PARTICK THISTLE v. AYR UNITED

9 May 1998   Scottish League First Division
Firhill Park   Attendance: 8,424

One week before this match, Falkirk had won 3-1 at Ayr. That defeat came at a time when Ayr United were flirting with relegation. The word 'flirting' has been carefully chosen to describe the situation. Elsewhere that afternoon, Stirling Albion sealed their relegation plight by losing 1-0 at home to St Mirren. It only remained for Partick Thistle to lose at Dundee and the First Division relegation issues would be resolved. Dundee had already won the championship and, even allowing for a lack of incentive, it was comfortably expected that Partick would suffer the defeat which would put them down too. Horrifyingly, the result was Dundee 0 Partick Thistle 3. Just as horrifying was the knowledge that the one game left was … Partick Thistle v. Ayr United! Flirting with relegation? Not any more. It was now perilous.

The situation was not complex. In order to escape, Ayr United required at least a draw. In order for Partick Thistle to escape, they had to win. At this time, many of the Ayr supporters were veterans of last-game escapes. This time though, there was a major difference – that of having to face the other team in peril. The only historical precedent for this was 1938, when Ayr United required at least a draw against a Dundee team which had to win. However, 1938 involved a different set of circumstances. At that time, unexpected developments elsewhere created a relegation scrap which only became apparent at half-time in the final game. In 1998, there was a whole week in which to worry about it.

In recognition of the importance of the occasion, the Ayr United board came up with the praiseworthy initiative of laying on free buses for the fans. Equally alive to what was at stake, the Partick Thistle supporters also turned up in impressive numbers, which meant the kick-off had to be delayed for fifteen minutes. It was even necessary to relocate home fans to an area of terracing which had long since been disused.

It was a day for strong nerves, although the reserves of courage threatened to be eroded by doubt. Was Partick Thistle's win over Dundee attributable to resurgent form or to the home team being having nothing to play for? Earlier in the season, Ayr United's visit to Firhill had resulted in a comprehensive 3-0 defeat against a fired-up home team. This time, the stakes were considerably higher.

Encouragingly, Ayr United created better chances in the opening part of the game. Ian Ferguson had a shot which went across the face of goal, and a further attack involved Billy Findlay hitting a drive which home goalkeeper Lindsay Hamilton touched over the crossbar. Then, with twenty-two minutes played, the home team won a free-kick, after Darren Henderson had been penalised in close proximity to the centre circle. What happened next was illustrative of the frayed nerves. The free-kick was taken in haste and was immediately intercepted by Ian Ferguson, who found himself with a clear run on the Partick Thistle goal, albeit that the run involved almost half of the length of the field. Instinctively, there was a feeling that the referee would find a reason to order a re-take. To get such a glorious opportunity from the opposition's free-kick seemed too good to be true. Play proceeded whilst the visiting fans rose to their feet in anticipation. It was a one-on-one situation, and the tension became increasingly unbearable as Ferguson ran ever further downfield. Lindsay Hamilton advanced from his goal and forced Ferguson to go wide. The fear now was whether the angle would be too acute, but it wasn't. The ball was slotted home amidst scenes and sounds of great exuberance.

Heavy pressure now lay upon a Partick Thistle team for whom not even a draw would suffice. Roared on by their rabid fans, they began to expend every effort in an attempt to pull

---

Partick Thistle 1   **Ayr United 3**
Evans   *Ferguson, Djaffo, Findlay*

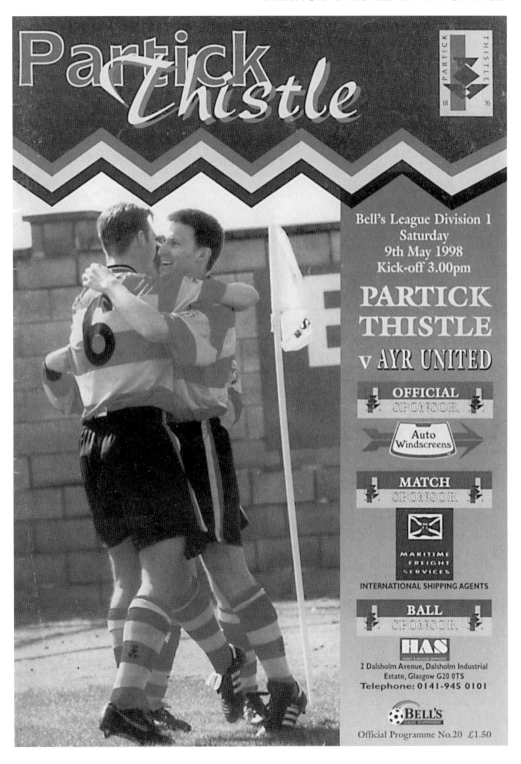

Bell's League Division 1
Saturday
9th May 1998
Kick-off 3.00pm

PARTICK THISTLE
v AYR UNITED

OFFICIAL SPONSOR

Auto Windscreens

MATCH SPONSOR

MARITIME FREIGHT SERVICES
INTERNATIONAL SHIPPING AGENTS

BALL SPONSOR

HAS
2 Dalsholm Avenue, Dalsholm Industrial
Estate, Glasgow G20 0TS
Telephone: 0141-945 0101

BELL'S
LEAGUE CHAMPIONSHIP

Official Programme No.20 £1.50

Partick Thistle v. Ayr United

League Goals 1997/98	
Djaffo	10
Ferguson	8
Kerrigan	3
Dick	2
Graham	2
Henderson	2
Millen	2
Traynor	2
Agnew	1
Anderson	1
Bell	1
Burns	1
Duthie	1
Findlay	1
Hood	1
Shepherd	1
Smith	1
Total	**40**

back from the brink of relegation. As half-time approached, it was hoped that the whistle would be blown with Ayr United still a goal to the good. In stoppage time, the home side mounted an ominous attack in which a Martin Lauchlan cross was cut back by Andy Lyons for Gareth Evans to make it 1-1 with a header. Firhill erupted. The proximity to the interval made this a sickening blow.

Six minutes into the second half, Gordon Dalziel made a substitution which proved to be a stroke of tactical genius. For Laurent Djaffo to perform to his potential, the occasion had to be right. The occasion *was* right, and he replaced Lou Donowa. The impact was as visible as it was immediate. Paul Shepherd crossed to Djaffo, who had his back to goal. The Frenchman expertly wheeled round and crashed a left-foot shot past Hamilton. He had been on the field for just five minutes.

The scoreline was now wholly satisfactory. Everything would be fine, unless Partick Thistle should score twice. More than half an hour remained, and it was anticipated that the Jags would be driven by desperation. If that desperation did exist, it seldom manifested itself in an attacking sense from this point on. Lindsay Hamilton, rather than David Castilla, proved to be the busier goalkeeper as the game progressed. Djaffo was the man who caused him to be so busy – the Partick defenders just could not cope with him. By dint of strength and skill, he was narrowly thwarted four times. Ian Ferguson shot too high from six yards, and a lob from Darren Henderson was well saved by Hamilton.

Partick Thistle looked beaten. In the closing minutes, it was not even remotely considered that they would get the requisite two goals. Billy Findlay made so bold as to embark on a solo run during stoppage time. He then parted with the ball, managing to strike it right into the roof of the net! It was a splendid conclusion to a fear-ridden occasion.

Partick Thistle: Hamilton, Boyle, Archibald, Watson, MacDonald, Stirling, Lauchlan, Henderson, Lawrence, Evans and Lyons. *Substitutes:* Martin, Nicolson and McKenzie.

Ayr United: Castilla, Shepherd, Miller, Millen, Traynor, Anderson, Donowa, Davies, Ferguson, Findlay and Henderson. *Substitutes:* Djaffo, Duthie and McKeown.

23 January 1999
Somerset Park

Scottish Cup Third Round
Attendance: 10,153

After suffering a Scottish Cup exit at Ayr in 1998, Kilmarnock manager Bobby Williamson claimed that he was gutted. How did he feel on being drawn to play at Ayr again in 1999? Gutted again? Perhaps not. It is just possible that he saw it as a perfect opportunity to atone for what had happened the year before. To Williamson's great credit, Kilmarnock sat second in the Premier League at the time of this tie. They had a six-point lead over Celtic and trailed Rangers by just four points. In addition to this, they had easily the best defensive record in the Premier League. There was no doubt that Killie's squad were capable of eradicating the memory of 1998. Yet the issue was not quite so straightforward as that. All connected to Ayr United had a burning desire for victory, and it was considered to be achievable when weighed up against Kilmarnock's perception that Somerset Park was inhospitable. The victory in 1998 had been in the 'plucky fighters' category. In 1999, the squad was possessed of sufficient flair to ensure that a further victory would not be similarly perceived.

In the opening stages, Killie's Ian Durrant was identified as a potent threat. His creative qualities made for some anxious moments. As early as the fourth minute, he floated in a corner-kick, which David Castilla punched away while under pressure. Further danger was visited on the Ayr goal when Gary Holt shot just past from an Ally McCoist lay-off. A series of Kilmarnock corners proved fruitless in the opening half-hour.

In his Ayr United career, Glynn Hurst did not score a Scottish Cup goal, but that statistic should not be allowed to mask his contribution to the club in this competition. This tie saw him at his pacey best; an attribute which assisted in the opening goal. It came in the twenty-ninth minute, when he cheekily lobbed the ball over Gus MacPherson, then darted past Kevin McGowne before laying it off to John Davies. A shot from Davies was firmly struck. It hit team-mate Andy Walker before breaking nicely to Andy Lyons, who drove it into the Kilmarnock net from near the edge of the penalty area. The ball had taken a deflection on the road in, but not sufficiently so to be classed as an own goal. The old derby passions were aroused as the fans and players celebrated excessively. By dint of tribal rivalries, Ayrshire derbies are not occasions when it is befitting to be modest in victory. Yet, when the clamour died down, it was necessary to face the practical reality that a considerable time had yet to be played. That reality was compounded when Kilmarnock staged a desperate pursuit of an equaliser.

In terms of pressure being applied, Kilmarnock's best phase of the game was the first half of the second half. The attacks came in waves, and each successfully repelled attack brought nothing more than temporary relief. Castilla's goal was persistently revisited in what emerged as an anxious part of the tie. Ally Mitchell connected well for a forty-ninth minute volley which went wide. Gary Holt struck a shot which would have been destined for the target, had the ball not got entangled in a sea of legs. Then, with sixty-nine minutes on the clock, Castilla pulled off a superb double-save. In mentioning these chances, this is far from an exhaustive summary of the pressure applied by the visitors during that spell.

Gradually, the pressure receded, and Ayr United re-emerged as an attacking force. With nine minutes remaining, the tie blew up. Glynn Hurst and Rae Montgomerie pursued a long ball. The Killie defender then pulled at Hurst's shirt, thereby dragging him to the ground. Referee Willie Young immediately pointed to the penalty spot. Montgomerie displayed vehement dissent at the decision. This was a yellow card offence to add to the one in the first half when he had caught Hurst late. Montgomerie was therefore sent off. In proof of the shirt

---

Ayr United 3
Lyons, Walker (2)

Kilmarnock 0

AYR UNITED v. KILMARNOCK

The second of Andy Walker's successful penalty kicks. The most frequently used adjective was 'audacious'.

pull, pictures later showed Hurst's number seven to have the illusion of being on the *front* of his shirt. 1-0 up with the ball on the penalty spot, less than ten minutes to go and the opposition reduced to ten men! It just remained for a successful penalty kick to strengthen the grip further. The man who placed the ball on the spot was Andy Walker. In front of him was Gordon Marshall, his former team-mate at Celtic. Behind Marshall were housed Ayr United's most partisan fans – the Somerset Road enders. Walker then blasted the ball home. At this point, the Somerset Road end did not have exclusive rights on partisanship. It was displayed in all the areas of the ground which accommodated Ayr support. Andy Walker wheeled away in obvious delight. The scene was one of general bedlam. The noise was raucous.

Two minutes later, Martin Baker brought down Gary Teale for another penalty kick. The excitement had not yet died down from the previous one. Again the responsibility was delegated to Andy Walker. It was wondered whether he would hit it in the same direction as the earlier one, or whether he would try something different. It transpired that something different was tried; *very* different. Afterwards, Andy Walker stated that, at the time of the second penalty, he believed that the tie was in the final minute. In truth, seven minutes plus some stoppage time remained. Anyway, what happened next found its way into local footballing folklore. He gently chipped the ball towards the middle of the goal and it seemed to float over the line like a feather. The assumption that Gordon Marshall would dive was correct. It could scarcely be believed that such a cheeky trick had been attempted. Andy Walker then wheeled away in the same direction as he had done two minutes earlier. With arms outstretched, he sprinted in the general direction of Tryfield Place. The fans had still been celebrating the goal before. This development added fresh impetus to these celebrations.

At 3-0, Ayr United continued to pile forward, and David Craig looked to be on the point of making it 4-0, but was closed down at the vital moment. Shortly afterwards, the final whistle blew on an excellent victory. The fans and the players acclaimed each other, whilst the familiar songs were sung with ever increasing gusto.

Ayr United: Castilla, Robertson, Winnie, Millen, Traynor, Craig, Hurst, Davies, Walker, Teale and Lyons. *Substitutes:* Reynolds, Welsh and Ferguson

Kilmarnock: Marshall, MacPherson, Montgomerie, McGowne, Baker, Reilly, Holt, Durrant, Roberts, McCoist and Mitchell. *Substitutes:* Mahood, Henry and Lauchlan.

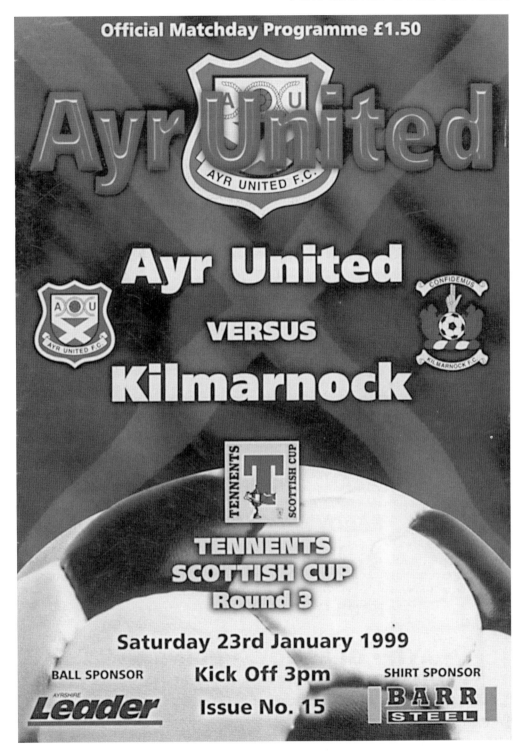

Official Matchday Programme £1.50

Ayr United
VERSUS
Kilmarnock

TENNENTS
SCOTTISH CUP
Round 3

Saturday 23rd January 1999

Kick Off 3pm

Issue No. 15

BALL SPONSOR

Leader
AYRSHIRE

SHIRT SPONSOR

BARR STEEL

AYR UNITED v. DUNDEE

15 February 2000   Scottish Cup Third Round Replay
Somerset Park   Attendance: 3,029

After a scoreless draw at Dens Park, the replay was the victim of a postponement less than an hour before the scheduled kick-off time. This was despite the Somerset Park pitch being perfectly playable. Referee Jim Herald saw fit to order the postponement due to the wind. One week later the replay proceeded, although the weather conditions meant that it came close to being abandoned. The elements made for a surreal atmosphere which, combined with Ayr United's first shoot-out at Somerset Park, heightened the sense of drama.

A disappointing attendance figure was understandable. It was an evening of bitter cold; the type of night which deterred all except the diehards. Something special was going to be needed to divert attention away from the rigours of a Scottish winter. The name of Glynn Hurst was synonymous with the expression 'blistering pace', and he was at his incisive best just two minutes into the tie. He got past two Dundee defenders, then unleashed a shot which was just a little too wide. A strong drive from Marvyn Wilson was on target, but Dundee goalkeeper Jamie Langfield managed to save it, albeit at the second attempt. Neither team was able to capitalise on any of the first-half chances created, but the scoreless situation did not undermine the competitiveness with which the tie was fought. The combative nature of play was illustrated by an incident in which Gavin Rae took out Neil Scally with a bad tackle, which caused the Dundee player to be shown a yellow card. Several minutes later, Scally was yellow-carded for attempting to wreak his own brand of revenge on Rae.

At half-time a fall of sleet descended on Somerset Park. As the second half progressed, the sleet gave way to snow and there was a rapid deterioration in conditions. The floodlights highlighted the snow to spectacular effect, but the picturesque spectacle was a secondary consideration in comparison with the threat of a postponement. Accelerating that threat was the sight of the line markings gradually disappearing. The only concession which the referee made to the conditions was the introduction of an orange ball in the seventy-ninth minute. It replaced the white ball, which had become camouflaged against the white surface.

At the end of ninety minutes, the nets had not been tested, and the referee pondered the possibility of abandoning the tie without recourse to extra time. A ten-minute delay permitted the lines to be swept and the snow had eased when the teams reappeared.

James Grady would eventually perform bold deeds for Ayr United but, in the colours of Dundee, he made ground down the left flank then crossed for Gavin Rae to shoot past Craig Nelson. This development took place inside the first minute of extra time. From this point on, Dundee grew in stature and the loss of a further goal began to look like a possibility. Then, in the closing minutes of the first period of extra time, so much authority was asserted that Dundee conceded four corner-kicks in quick succession. The last in that series involved Gary Teale crossing for Neil Duffy to make it 1-1 from a glancing header.

There was almost a dramatic development in the final minute of the second period of extra time. Glynn Hurst managed to round the Dundee goalkeeper, but his shot was off-target. Shortly afterwards, the whistle blew to signify that the contest would be decided by a test of nerve. A kick-by-kick summary of the shootout follows:

James Grady scored for Dundee – 0-1; Neil Duffy scored for Ayr – 1-1;
Willie Falconer scored for Dundee – 1-2; David Craig scored for Ayr – 2-2;

Ayr United 1   **Dundee 1** (after extra time)
Duffy   *Rae*

Ayr United won 7-6 on kicks from the penalty mark

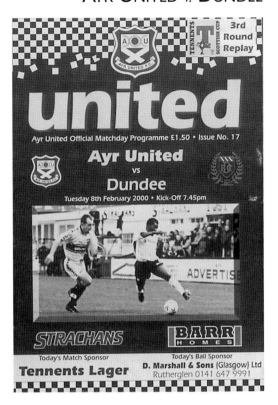

Note that the programme cover carried the date originally scheduled.

Craig Nelson saved from Gavin Rae of Dundee – 2-2; Jamie Langfield saved from Roddy Grant of Ayr – 2-2;
Lee Sharp scored for Dundee – 2-3; Glynn Hurst scored for Ayr – 3-3;
Lee Wilkie scored for Dundee – 3-4; Marvyn Wilson scored for Ayr – 4-4.

This put it to the sudden death stage.

Robbie Raeside scored for Dundee – 4-5; Gary Teale scored for Ayr – 5-5;
Barry Smith scored for Dundee – 5-6; Paul Shepherd scored for Ayr – 6-6;
Craig Nelson saved from Nicky Banger of Dundee – 6-6; John Robertson scored for Ayr– 7-6.

The kicks from Marvyn Wilson, Gary Teale and Paul Shepherd had to be scored merely to stay in the tie. It is also worth recalling that there was a phase of eight consecutive successful kicks. A close look at the Dundee scorers reveals the names of three players who would eventually play for Ayr United. The names are James Grady, Willie Falconer (played for Ayr United in friendlies only) and Lee Sharp. Hugh Robertson and Steven Boyack were also destined to play for Ayr United.

It was fortunate that the shoot-out took place at the favoured Somerset Road end. Understandably, John Robertson sparked wild scenes of jubilation with that final kick.

Ayr United: Nelson, McMillan, Robertson, Scally, Craig, Duffy, Teale, Wilson, Hurst, Tarrant and Shepherd. *Substitutes:* Grant, Crilly and Reynolds.
Dundee: Langfield, Smith, McSkimming, Robertson, Tweed, Raeside, Boyack, Rae, Bayne, Wilkie and Falconer. *Substitutes:* Grady, Banger and Sharp.

MOTHERWELL v. AYR UNITED

26 February 2000
Fir Park

Scottish Cup Fourth Round
Attendance: 5,222

Prior to this tie, there had only been one other occasion when Ayr United had pulled off an away Scottish Cup win against a club from a higher League (on 15 February 1964). Nevertheless, there were high hopes of overcoming the challenge of Motherwell. In the two previous seasons, Kilmarnock had been eliminated from the competition at Somerset Park, and Dundee had suffered the same fate in 2000. This was ample proof that Ayr had the ability to conquer Premier League opposition in the Scottish Cup. This time, of course, ground advantage was not a factor, and there was the additional fact that Motherwell were sitting in third place in the Premier League.

The tie had hardly settled when the scoring action began. Mickey Reynolds hared up the right flank, then crossed for Gary Teale to beat Andy Goram with a low volley. Soon there was a threat to that lead. Team-mates Craig Nelson and John Robertson collided with each other with potentially catastrophic results. Nelson left the field for seven minutes, during which time he received sixteen stitches and two pain-killing injections. Full-back Robertson took temporary charge of the gloves, thereby rekindling memories of the match at Dundee's Dens Park in April 1998, when he had saved a penalty. As full-backs go, John Robertson was a good goalkeeper! However, the situation was fraught with danger, even although he managed to keep the Motherwell forwards at bay.

Ironically, a goal was conceded immediately after the temporary incumbent had handed back the gloves to Craig Nelson. This happened when a Kevin Twaddle corner-kick was prodded over the line by McCulloch. At least, that is what the officials considered to have happened. There was a dispute about whether or not the ball actually crossed the line. Television evidence indicated that a goal should not have been given. This incident happened in the twenty-second minute. Seven minutes later, Kevin Twaddle crossed from the left and Don Goodman rushed in to shoot high into the net from three yards – this tie still had plenty of life left in it. Three minutes later, Mickey Reynolds was brought down by Jamie McGowan and a penalty kick was awarded. Andy Goram dived in the opposite direction enabling Gary Teale's attempt from the spot to make it 2-2 with marginally more than half an hour on the clock. Yet again, three minutes elapsed until the next goal and, yet again, it was a penalty kick. Don Goodman was adjudged to have been tripped by Craig Nelson, and the referee unhesitatingly pointed to the spot. Ged Brannan did what was required of him, but the goal flurry was not yet complete. This time, the time lapse until the next goal was four minutes. Neil Tarrant found himself isolated at the edge of the Motherwell penalty area. He opted to go for glory with a low drive. It was a sensible option because he succeeded in planting the ball behind Goram. Six minutes remained until half-time and the score had a remarkable air about it at 3-3.

In the post-match analysis, it was generally considered that the high scoring was attributable to both teams having the courage to play two conventional wingers each; Gary Teale and Mickey Reynolds for Ayr and Kevin Twaddle and Derek Townsley for Motherwell. At half-time, it was wondered whether the scoring would continue unabated. As it turned out, it died down in the second half, although there were talking points aplenty after the break. In the fifty-ninth minute, Neil Tarrant drove Ayr United in front after Gary Teale and Glynn Hurst had created the chance. There was a spontaneous outburst of joy from the travelling support. Four minutes later, the joy turned to despair. In the first half, Mickey Reynolds had

Motherwell 3
McCulloch, Goodman, Brannan

Ayr United 4
Teale (2), Tarrant (2)

Above: Andy McMillan's beautifully clean shirt proves to be the envy of his mud-stained opponent.

Right: Programme cover.

Gary Teale closes in.

MOTHERWELL v. AYR UNITED

Neil Tarrant is at the head of the queue for the ball.

been yellow-carded, along with Motherwell's Stephen McMillan, for an altercation between the pair. Now he found himself in the situation of being spoken to by the referee for a tackle on Pat Nevin. The tackle was far from the bone-crunching variety, but Nevin's reaction conveyed a contrary impression. Whether justified, or not, Mickey Reynolds was shown a red card. The potential consequences were grim. With close to half an hour left, it was necessary for the fourth bottom club in the First Division to soldier on with ten men on the ground of the third-placed club in the Premier Division.

In an attempt to at least force a replay, Motherwell committed two more substitutes to exhaust their permitted quota. One of them was former Ayr United player John Davies, brother of Motherwell manager Billy Davies. With several minutes left, Stephen McMillan limped off with a foot injury, the consequence being that numerical parity was restored. Yet that did not dilute the burning desire to hear the final whistle. It was sounded with the lead still intact.

In 1953, a League fixture had also finished with a scoreline of Motherwell 3 Ayr United 4, but there was a greater reward for the victory in 2000. That reward was being drawn at home to Partick Thistle in the quarter-final. After safely negotiating that stage with a 2-0 win, the club entered the semi-final of the Scottish Cup for the first time since 1973 and only the second time ever.

Motherwell: Goram, Doesburg, McGowan, Denham, McMillan, Townsley, Brannan, Valakari, Twaddle, Goodman and McCulloch. *Substitutes:* Nevin, Davies and Nicholas.

Ayr United: Nelson, McMillan, Shepherd, Craig, Robertson, Duffy, Wilson, Tarrant, Reynolds, Teale and Hurst. *Substitutes:* Crilly, Grant and Campbell.

AYR UNITED v. KILMARNOCK

9 October 2001
Somerset Park

CIS Cup Third Round
Attendance: 7,418

At the time of the draw, there was a certain amount of trepidation. This was due to a combination of adverse form in the First Division and the fear that Kilmarnock would come to Ayr thirsting for revenge. They had much to seek revenge for. Their promotion to the Premier League had caused the cessation of Ayrshire rivalry at League level, but habitual pairings in Cup competitions renewed that rivalry. Taking stock of the situation, Ayr United entered this tie with memories of having eliminated Kilmarnock from the Coca-Cola Cup in 1996/97 and the Scottish Cup in both 1997/98 and 1998/99. The supporters were also aware of the concept of arithmetical progression since the victorious scorelines were, in chronological order, 1-0, 2-0 and 3-0. This gave rise to suggestions that Ayr United were going to win 4-0, not that the suggestions carried a great deal of conviction. In reality, the tie was approached with a distinct hope of going through by any margin at all.

The absence of such influential players as David Craig and Pat McGinlay did not have an unduly detrimental effect in the early stages. Right from the start, an attacking approach was adopted and a high level of self-belief was evident. Kilmarnock hit on the counter attack in the seventh minute. Gary McCutcheon managed to evade John Robertson before cutting the ball back to Ally Mitchell, who attempted a shot which Paul Sheerin blocked. Four minutes later, Eddie Annand crossed, but Martin Baker effected a timely clearance to thwart Gary Teale, the intended recipient. Yet Kilmarnock too showed that they knew how to attack. During this spell of the tie, Craig Nelson had to deal with a couple of shots from Ally Mitchell.

In the twenty-seventh minute, Kilmarnock were desperately lucky to keep their goal intact. Gordon Marshall committed himself to a Gary Teale cross, which he failed to claim. This allowed James Grady to get in a shot which was unwittingly diverted wide by team-mate Eddie Annand. Soon afterwards, Annand was in the act of bursting clear on Gordon Marshall when Martin Baker tripped him. Referee Willie Young took no action. With three minutes of the first half left, no such leniency was shown to Paul Sheerin, who was sent off for supposedly stamping on Andy McLaren, who had committed a bad tackle. McLaren was booked for his part in the incident and, from this point on, the home crowd jeered every time he touched the ball.

As the second half progressed, the respective goalkeepers were called upon to make routine saves. The tie then started to witness some alarming developments as Kilmarnock began to step up their attacking emphasis and, suddenly, the loss of Paul Sheerin looked to be having a major impact. The occasional counter-attack was made possible by the pace of Gary Teale, although such relief was nothing more than temporary at this stage of the tie. Then, in the eighty-eighth minute, Ally Mitchell crossed to give young Kilmarnock substitute Kris Boyd what looked like a simple chance to score what would have been a certain winner. The task required of him was to nod the ball into a vacant net from six yards. Boyd made good contact with the header. Miraculously, though, his downward header was too firm. The ball struck the ground with such force that it bounced over the crossbar. It was scarcely believable that the ball had failed to end up nestling in the net. In the ninetieth minute, a McLaren cross provided Boyd with a further chance for glory, but this time the header was well wide.

The changing course of the game indicated that extra time was not an alluring prospect from the Ayr United viewpoint. Any fears were far from dispelled. From the onset of extra

---

Ayr United 0

Kilmarnock 0 (after extra time)

Ayr United won 5-4 on kicks from the penalty mark

Chris Innes squats dejectedly after his decsive penalty miss. Craig McEwan leads the celebrating Ayr players. He is followed by Eddie Annand, Marvyn Wilson (background) and John Bradford.

time, Kilmarnock maintained the attacking impetus. It was now futile to contemplate what might have developed had Paul Sheerin remained on the field. The emphasis was on compact defending and the hope of something special happening on the break. Boyd, Dargo, McLaren and Innes were all prominent in getting in attempts on the Ayr goal during extra time. Still the defence stood firm. Right to the end of the concluding period of added time, the pressure was applied. Then came the final whistle. The teams were now even, since the loss of a player could have no bearing on a shoot-out. Indeed, there was even an element of advantage, since it was to be staged at the Somerset Road end. This is what happened next.

Lee Sharp scored for Ayr – 1-0; Frederic Dindeleux scored for Kilmarnock – 1-1; Gordon Marshall saved from Ayr's Brian McLaughlin – 1-1; Alan Mahood scored for Kilmarnock – 1-2;
Craig McEwan scored for Ayr – 2-2; Andy McLaren scored for Kilmarnock – 2-3;
John Bradford scored for Ayr – 3-3; Kris Boyd scored for Kilmarnock – 3-4;
Eddie Annand scored for Ayr – 4-4; Craig Nelson saved from Kilmarnock's Craig Dargo – 4-4.

This put it to the sudden death stage. Neil Duffy scored for Ayr – 5-4; Chris Innes of Kilmarnock hit the ball over – 5-4. Craig Nelson was a particular hero of the shoot-out. Ayr United would have been out had he failed to save from Craig Dargo. Yet the abiding memory was the sight of the final kick, which saw the ball bound for the direction of the night sky. Victory had been achieved, despite being a man short for seventy-eight minutes.

Ayr United: Nelson, Robertson, Lovering, Duffy, Hughes, Sheerin, Teale, Wilson, Annand, Grady and Sharp. *Substitutes:* McLaughlin, Bradford, McEwan, Smyth and Dodds.
Kilmarnock: Marshall, Canero, Mitchell, Mahood, Baker, Dindeleux, Dargo, McLaren, Innes, Calderon and McCutcheon. *Substitutes:* Pizzo, Boyd, Hessey, Di Giacomo and Stewart.

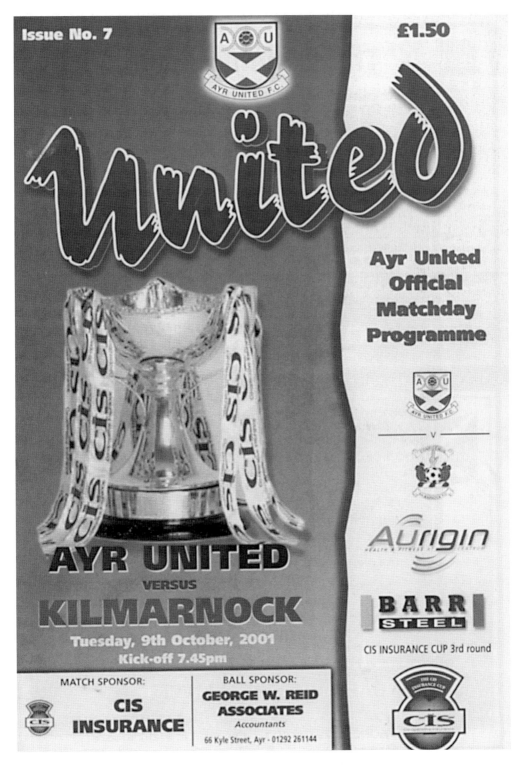

Issue No. 7

£1.50

Ayr United
Official
Matchday
Programme

AYR UNITED

VERSUS

KILMARNOCK

Tuesday, 9th October, 2001
Kick-off 7.45pm

A U
AYR UNITED F.C.

v

Aurigin
HEALTH & FITNESS

BARR
STEEL

CIS INSURANCE CUP 3rd round

MATCH SPONSOR:

CIS
INSURANCE

BALL SPONSOR:

GEORGE W. REID
ASSOCIATES
Accountants
66 Kyle Street, Ayr - 01292 261144

HIBS v. AYR UNITED

6 February 2002   CIS Cup Semi-Final
Hampden Park   Attendance: 11,779

In reflection of the sponsorship, the competition was termed the CIS Cup but, under the original guise of the League Cup, Ayr United had been unsuccessful at the semi-final stage in seasons 1950/51, 1969/70 and 1980/81. This time, the semi-final ballot saw the club pitched in along with Rangers, Celtic and Hibs and, by avoiding the Old Firm, a reasonable chance of progressing to the final was afforded. In the time between the draw being made and the tie taking place, Hibs manager Alex McLeish moved to Rangers to take up the managerial post. His replacement, Franck Sauzee, struggled to get results, thereby giving rise to a belief that there was a genuine chance of beating Hibs. Then, on the Saturday prior to this Wednesday evening tie, Hibs put up a splendid peformance to draw with runaway League leaders Celtic. The question as to whether Ayr United could progress to a major cup final for the first time ever, however, remained in abeyance.

The first shot of the night fell to Pat McGinlay, who fired the ball high over the Hibs crossbar. Yet these opening minutes predominantly required defensive qualities to be shown. A cross from Ulises de la Cruz was dealt with by Neil Duffy heading over his own bar. This happened with just five minutes on the clock, and it was a development which indicated that the Ayr United defence would perhaps be on the brink of a busy shift. Grant Brebner tested Craig Nelson with a shot which he saved but failed to hold, and David Craig was on hand to apply a clearance. Craig Nelson had to be alert again to stop a drive from John O'Neil. However, these attacks were countered by Marvyn Wilson laying off a free-kick to Paul Sheerin, who shot just over the Hibs bar. Midway through the first half, James Grady beat Paul Fenwick to a ball from Eddie Annand, then shot for the top corner of the Hibs net. Goalkeeper Nick Colgan matched the shot with a good save.

As the half progressed, Ayr United began to assume the ascendancy. An important factor was the inspirational figure of captain John 'Yogi' Hughes. His promptings ensured that there would be no slacking. Shortly before the interval, John Robertson burst into the Hibs penalty area where a challenge from Paul Fenwick resulted in the ball bouncing hard off Robbo's face. It was fortunate that he was made of stern stuff.

Prior to the tie, it was considered that Ulises de la Cruz would be a troublesome opponent. He was Hibs' most expensive signing ever, and had made more than fifty appearances for Ecuador. After making little impression, he was substituted in the twelfth minute of the second half. Two minutes afterwards, Eddie Annand released Pat McGinlay, who found himself clean through on Colgan. McGinlay connected well, but his drive was too straight and the goalkeeper saved it. This scare seemed to stir Hibs out of their lethargy and a David Zitelli header was just a little wide. The Ayr defence grew in stature. John Hughes, David Craig and Neil Duffy soaked up whatever came their way, whilst John Robertson and Paul Lovering were both strong in the tackle and quick on the overlap. Behind them, Craig Nelson simply oozed confidence.

With eighty minutes played, a Paul Sheerin corner-kick was cleared in the direction of John Hughes, but 'Yogi' fired the ball over. Such raids indicated that there was a capability of winning. The capability became a possibility when a free-kick was won in close proximity to the Hibs penalty area. It was known that a goal at this time would have been a certain winner, and the noisy Ayr supporters roared encouragement while awaiting the outcome with keen anticipation. However, the anticipation was in vain. Referee Mike McCurry blew the final whistle before the kick could be taken.

Hibs 0   Ayr United 1 (after extra time)
                                Annand

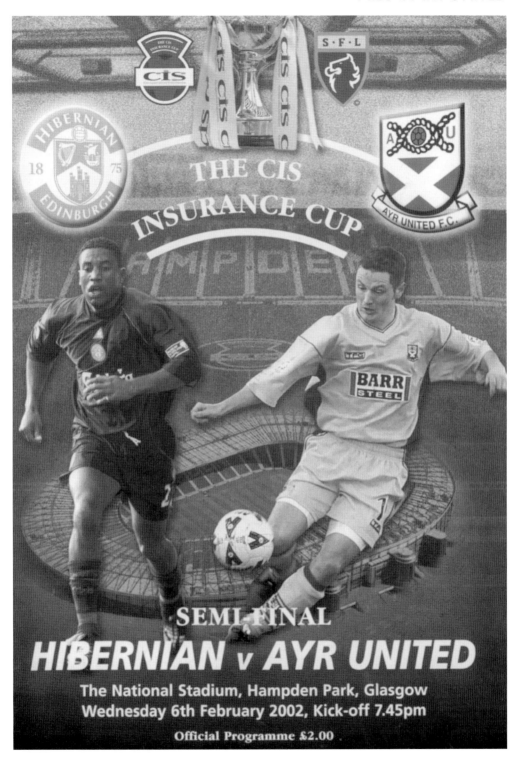

THE CIS
INSURANCE CUP

SEMI-FINAL
HIBERNIAN v AYR UNITED
The National Stadium, Hampden Park, Glasgow
Wednesday 6th February 2002, Kick-off 7.45pm
Official Programme £2.00

HIBS v. AYR UNITED

In the early minutes of extra time, a John Robertson cross was won by Pat McGinlay, whose header went wide. A subsequent attack saw a McGinlay attempt hit the side netting. Maybe, just maybe, one of those forays into Hibs territory would eventually bring the reward of a goal. With eleven minutes of extra time on the clock, Neil Scally put through an incisive pass. John Robertson latched onto it and made ground inside the Hibs box before being pushed in the back by Ian Murray. It was a sensational development, which resulted in a penalty-kick being awarded. Great excitement broke out amongst the Ayr support, although it was tempered with the knowledge that the kick had yet to be converted. The tension was difficult to bear when Eddie Annand placed the ball on the spot. During the run-up, the tension momentarily heightened further. The culmination was a spontaneous outburst of wild celebration as the ball was expertly sent to the top corner of the net.

It was hardly a time for calm reflection. Ayr United had lost a lead at advanced stages of each of the three semi-finals they had previously played in this competition, but it is doubtful whether historical precedent was on the minds of many supporters at this stage of the Hibs tie. Lusty renditions of favourite songs rose into the night air, whilst the yellow-clad Ayr players set about maintaining the slender lead.

During the second period of extra time, Hibs piled forward consistently only to be met by a resolute wall of defenders, all of whom shared the concentrated aim of winning the tie without recourse to a shoot-out. Each tackle and clearance was cheered, as the game progressed on its seemingly interminable course. At last the scoreboard clocks reached thirty minutes. Surely now the final whistle would relieve the agony. Amidst the clamour, relatively few would have heard it, but the referee's gesture was apparent to all. Equally apparent was the consequence of it all.

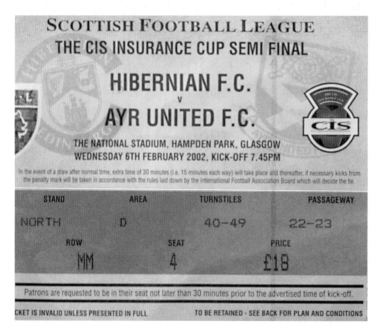

Match ticket.

Marvyn Wilson evades Alen Orman, Hibs' Bosnian midfielder. Paul Lovering is in the background.

'Super Ayr' and similar renditions lifted into the night sky, whilst the players and staff were in equally celebratory mood. Some of the post-match analysis indicated that the tie had been a poor spectacle. These critics would have seen the game from a totally different perspective had they viewed it from within the midst of the excited spectators who were housed in the North Stand.

In the dying seconds, Eddie Annand had broken clear in a counter-attack, only to pull up sharply with a bit of hamstring trouble. He had already been booked in the match and this, combined with a booking earlier in the competition, meant that he was banned for the final; a considerably greater agony than a hamstring pull. Yet Eddie Annand managed to write his name large in the history of Ayr United. He was the scorer of a goal which ended a wait of close to ninety-two years.

Ayr United: Nelson, Robertson, Lovering, Duffy, Hughes, Craig, Wilson, McGinlay, Annand, Grady and Sheerin. *Substitutes:* Scally, Sharp, McLaughlin, McEwan and Dodds.

Hibs: Colgan, de la Cruz, Murray, Brebner, O'Neil, Fenwick, Wiss, Smith, Zitelli, O'Connor and Caldwell. *Substitutes:* Orman, Hurtado, O'Riordan, Caig and Townsley.

RANGERS v. AYR UNITED

17 March 2002   CIS Cup Final
Hampden Park   Attendance: 50,076

At first glance it may be wondered why a 4-0 defeat against Rangers falls under the 'classic match' category. Yet readers must understand that the scoreline was harsh and that this was Ayr United's first appearance in a major cup final.

The public took the importance of the occasion to heart. This much was evidenced by the fact that the club sold out a ticket allocation which exceeded 12,000. Entire families made plans to travel, while exiled fans flew in from various corners of the globe. Local shops competed for the best 'Ayr United' window display, whilst scarves, hats, flags and face-paints sold briskly. In the build-up, there was a media focus on Ayr United supporters going to Hampden for 'a great day out'. Admittedly, there was a veneer of frivolity, but there was also some serious business to see to.

The teams emerged to a noisy welcome, whilst a prevalence of black-and-white flags added splendour to the occasion. Had there been any justice, Eddie Annand would have been in the line-up. There was little scope for argument concerning the two bookings which caused his ban from the final. It just seemed tough that the bookings were months apart. Also, in order to reach the final, Ayr United had played a round more than Rangers. This created more time in which to accumulate the bookings. Neither was Scott Crabbe available for selection. He was cup-tied, having already played in the competition for Raith Rovers.

The game was not allowed a settling-in period. Paul Lovering came close to scoring with little more than a minute played. His shock was struck with power and Stefan Klos was no doubt relieved to see the ball clear his left-hand post. With just four minutes on the clock, David Craig cleared a threatening situation at the opposite end. With Craig Nelson stranded, he effected a strong clearance from an effort by Claudio Caniggia. Just two minutes later, the Ayr goal was again under threat. Caniggia struck a low cross into the six-yard box, and Peter Lovenkrands managed to ghost between John Robertson and John Hughes to get a shot in. Nelson saved it brilliantly at point-blank range. The time lapse to the next piece of excitement was again two minutes. Near the halfway line, Tony Vidmar misjudged the ball, thereby allowing Brian McLaughlin a clear run on the Rangers goal. McLaughlin hared down the field, while the Ayr supporters rose to their feet in anticipation. Vidmar raced in hot pursuit before getting in a saving tackle to atone for his error.

As the game progressed, it became obvious that Rangers were capable of being matched or even outmatched. Then came an agonising development in the twenty-ninth minute. Stefan Klos was off his line when Brian McLaughlin attempted a measured chip. The ball floated over the goalkeeper and the crowd noise prompted McLaughlin to turn and acclaim a goal. Yet somehow Klos, after looking beaten, managed to dive back and claw the ball out. It was a dreadful disappointment, although it encouraged the Ayr crowd towards a few more lusty renditions. It was not long before these same voices were expressing anger. Pat McGinlay was brought down in the penalty area by Arthur Numan, but no penalty was awarded. Within a minute, McGinlay hit a long-range drive which Klos touched over. By now, an Ayr United win was becoming an increasing possibility. There was a scare when Peter Lovenkrands went down in the Ayr box. The momentary fright subsided when referee Hugh Dallas correctly interpreted the action as a dive. Two minutes from half-time, Rangers scored. Caniggia put through a ball which Tore Andre Flo shot across the face of goal and it went in off a post. To this point of the match, Flo had been relatively anonymous.

Rangers 4   Ayr United 0
Flo, Ferguson, Caniggia (2)

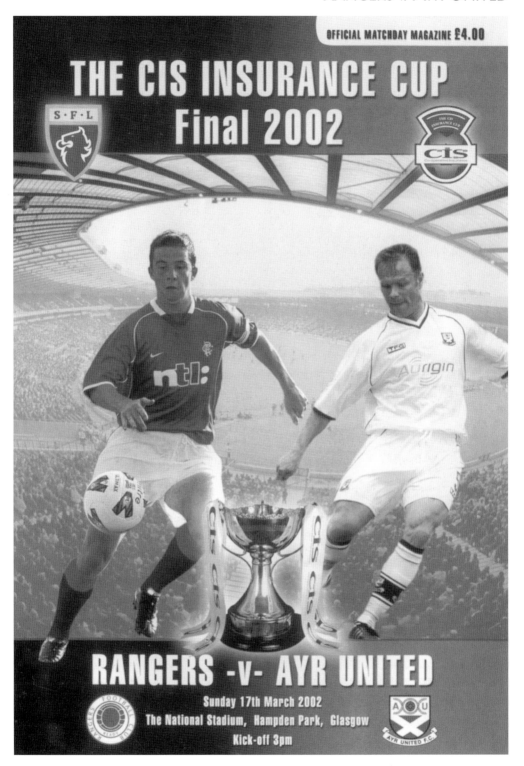

Rangers v. Ayr United

On the balance of play, the loss of this goal was deemed to be an injustice, although there could be no dispute as to the legitimacy of the strike. The same could not be said about a goal which came in the third minute of the second half. A Paul Lovering tackle on Russell Latapy resulted in the little Trinidadian going down. Amongst the many reports of the incident were such descriptions as: 'He went down like a Saturday coupon' and 'Latapy went down in theatrical style'. Some of the people seated in the vicinity of the author were less delicate in expressing their opinions on the award of a penalty. Barry Ferguson made it 2-0 from the spot.

At the other end, Lorenzo Amoruso brought down James Grady in the box. It should have been a stonewall penalty award but, cynically or not, it might be observed that the Ayr support experienced no great surprise at play being allowed to continue.

Left: From left to right: John Hughes, Barry Ferguson, Paul Sheerin, Brian McLaughlin, Craig Nelson, Neil McCann, Pat McGinlay, Russell Latapy, Bert Konterman and Marvyn Wilson.

Below: Match ticket.

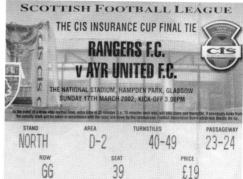

Earlier on, there had been so much promise yet, in the closing stages, the match gradually degenerated into a lost cause. Quarter of an hour remained when Caniggia volleyed home a cross from Neil McCann. In the final minute, the Argentinian scored again, this time with a header from a Fernando Ricksen cross. It was perhaps typical of Ayr United's luck that this goal too was in dispute. Neil Duffy made a frantic attempt to prevent the ball from crossing the line. Television pictures were unable to confirm that he had failed to do so.

It was now time to put the flags, hats and face-paints away until Ayr United's next big Hampden occasion … six days later!

Rangers: Klos, Ricksen, Vidmar, Amoruso, Numan, Ferguson, Caniggia, Konterman, Flo, Latapy and Lovenkrands. *Substitutes:* Hughes, Dodds, McCann, Kanchelskis and McGregor.

Ayr United: Nelson, Robertson, Lovering, Duffy, Hughes, Craig, Wilson, McGinlay, McLaughlin, Grady and Sheerin. *Substitutes:* Kean, Chaplain, McEwan, Sharp and Dodds.

AYR UNITED v. CELTIC

23 March 2002
Hampden Park

Scottish Cup Semi-Final
Attendance: 26,774

The First Division status of Ayr United was belied in the 2001/02 season. In reaching the final of the CIS Cup, two Premier League clubs, Kilmarnock and Hibs, were eliminated. Similarly, in progressing to the last four of the Scottish Cup, another two Premier League clubs were beaten en route. These clubs were Dunfermline Athletic and Dundee United. This gave rise to a justifiable belief that the club could acquit itself more satisfactorily against the Old Firm than average Premier League clubs.

The Celtic tie comprised Ayr United's third match at Hampden since 6 February and the second tie there that week. By this time, the route to Hampden was well known, although this gave rise to a familiarity which diluted the anticipation. Only in 1973 and 2000 had the club previously reached this stage of the Scottish Cup but, on this occasion, the sense of novelty was missing. Yet that did not prevent the fans from providing loud vocal backing yet again. There was much to sing about.

Illustrative of the course of the tie was that goalkeeper Craig Nelson had less work during the ninety minutes than Rab Douglas, his Celtic counterpart. Also, the fact that an Ayr United forward, James Grady, picked up the Man Of The Match award was yet more proof that an earnest attempt was made to defeat Celtic. Gordon Dalziel managed to instill in his players a self-belief, which permitted them to control the flow during long periods of this tie. It was difficult to believe that the team consistently made light of the best team in Scotland.

The state of the Hampden pitch had been the topic of much adverse publicity, although it did not prevent the yellow-clad Ayr players from tearing into Celtic with a brand of neat, fluent football. As early as the fourth minute, a free-kick was conceded for a Marvyn Wilson challenge on Stilian Petrov. The range was about twenty yards, and there were some tense moments when Henrik Larsson was making his run-up. There was relief when the ball sailed well over the top. The tension was misplaced. Fraught moments were to be relatively few in the eighty-six remaining minutes.

John Robertson was dangerous on the overlap throughout and, in the fourteenth minute, he did well to get in a shot of which Rab Douglas was the equal. John Hartson shot wide of the Ayr goal midway through the first half and repeated the feat a minute later. Then, with less than half an hour played, Celtic's Steve Guppy had to be substituted due to a knock he had taken. The Ayr United cause would have been better served if Guppy had remained on. His replacement, Alan Thompson, would ultimately prove hugely influential in the outcome of the tie.

Beforehand, a 0-0 half-time scoreline would have been considered more than satisfactory but, after a postive first half, it was greeted with a disbelief that Ayr United were not in front. Chances created included Paul Lovering hitting the sidenet and Pat McGinlay shooting wide after being set up by James Grady, who had dispossessed Neil Lennon. These chances paled into insignificance in comparison to what happened four minutes before the break. A long goalkick from Craig Nelson caught Celtic defender Bobo Balde in a state of indecision. James Grady, in contrast, was totally decisive. He nipped in and got a foot to the ball. By now the Ayr supporters were on their feet. Rab Douglas was off his line and the ball was rolling in the direction of an unguarded goal, but it went wide by a matter of inches. It was wretched luck. Before the half-time whistle, the Celtic goal came close to being breached again. Paul Sheerin unleashed a vicious drive, which Douglas could only punch out.

Ayr United 0

Celtic 3
Larsson, Thompson (2)

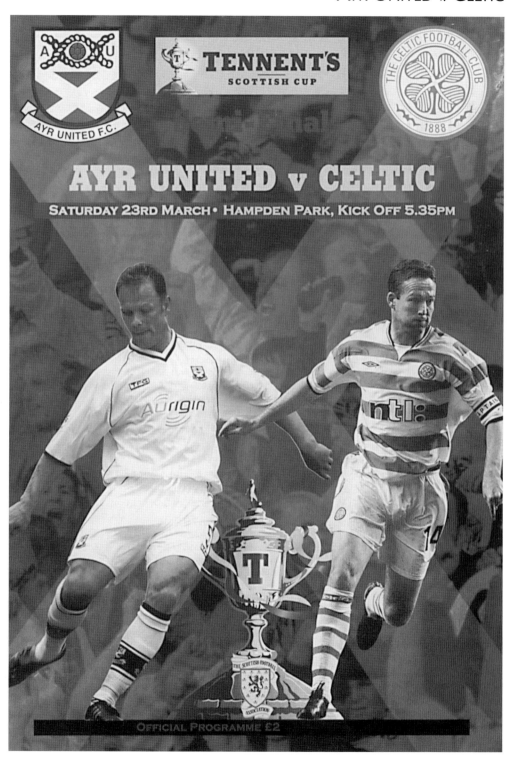

TENNENT'S
SCOTTISH CUP

THE CELTIC FOOTBALL CLUB
1888

AYR UNITED F.C.

AYR UNITED v CELTIC

SATURDAY 23RD MARCH • HAMPDEN PARK, KICK OFF 5.35PM

OFFICIAL PROGRAMME £2

James Grady's near miss, several minutes before the interval.

During the break, the fans seriously contemplated winning the tie. Three minutes into the second half, there was a threat to that ambition. Neil Lennon released Didier Agathe, who got past Paul Lovering during his advance on goal. In the first half, Agathe had been booed for displaying an irritating trait of hitting the ground too easily when challenged. Yet again, there was the threat of losing a free-kick in a key position, and perhaps this explained the absence of a firm tackle. Agathe made his way along the by-line, then delivered a low cross which Henrik Larsson latched onto in a flash before scoring.

There was a positive response to this reverse. In midfield, Celtic's Petrov, Lambert and Lennon remained stifled by Marvyn Wilson, Pat McGinlay and Paul Sheerin. Celtic were quite simply not allowed to settle on their 1-0 lead. With sixty-six minutes played, Eddie Annand went on for Scott Crabbe. Three minutes later, he cut the ball back to James Grady, who crashed it against the crossbar. Television revealed that Douglas had got a slight touch; perhaps just enough to deflect what would otherwise have been a goal. Grady had gone so close to putting Ayr United ahead in the first half, and now he found himself in the situation of going even closer to scoring an equaliser. It was scarcely credible that the stadium scoreboards still showed Celtic to be winning 1-0. The Ayr United players began to smell blood.

Pat McGinlay was not a respecter of Henrik Larsson's reputation.

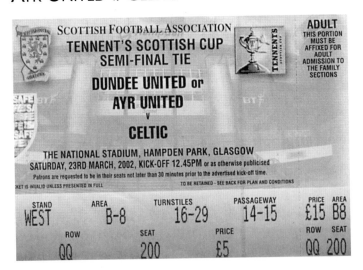

Match ticket.

This was a season in which Celtic managed to beat such European giants as Ajax and Juventus, as well as sweeping to the Premier League title in emphatic style. In this tie though, their defence began to look distinctly vulnerable, and James Grady was soon back to test his old Dundee team-mate, who palmed out the powerful drive.

In the eighty-first minute, there was a killer blow. Paul Sheerin tackled Didier Agathe who, expectedly, hit the ground. Alan Thompson took the free-kick and the ball screamed into the net via the underside of the crossbar. Post-match analysis correctly hailed this as a wonder goal. Yet it may have been more appropriate had the post-match analysis shown a a bit more focus on the award of the free-kick. Three minutes remained when Thompson again scored. Ayr United did not deserve to lose at all. For Celtic to win 3-0 was an injustice which even their manager, Martin O'Neill, admitted.

Ayr United: Nelson, Robertson, Lovering, Duffy, Hughes, Craig, Wilson, McGinlay, Crabbe, Grady and Sheerin. *Substitutes:* McLaughlin, Annand, McEwan, Sharp and Dodds.
Celtic: Douglas, Mjallby, Balde, Crainey, Agathe, Lambert, Lennon, Petrov, Guppy, Larsson and Hartson. *Substitutes:* Thompson, McNamara, Gould, Boyd and Moravcik.